The Jack Russell Terrier: Canine Companion Or Demon Dog

The Ultimate Guide to Training, Showing, and Living with a Jack Russell Terrier

By Don and Kellie Rainwater

Contents

Chapter 1

The History of Jack Russell Terriers

Jack Russell's are a short stocky breed originating from Britain. Today's Jack Russell's are characterized by two-tone or tri-color patterns of white, brown, and sometimes black. Modern day Jack Russell's are also much more sturdy and muscled than their ancestors.

The breed was originally known as the Fox Terrier. The breed was renamed in the late 1800's for the world renowned hunting enthusiast, Reverend John Russell. Russell was born in 1795 into a devoutly religious family that lived in the countryside of Dartmouth, England. Russell was educated at Blundell's School and would later attend Oxford University. By 1814 the nineteen year old Russell was associating with the nobles and aristocrats of England. It was at this time that the young man was invited to his first fox hunting expedition with a group that was led by the late Earl of Fortescue. Russell immediately fell in love with the sport fox hunting which would develop into a lifelong obsession. It was shortly after that the young man developed a keen interest in the breeds of dog often used by Fox hunting enthusiasts, in particular the Fox Terrier.

Russell had a passion and understanding for the breed that is still highly regarded today. In the Fox Terrier, Russell saw the potential to create the world's finest hunting dog. By 1830 Russell would establish an intensive breeding program in order to create a breed that would meet the needs of any British hunter.

It is said that while he was still at Oxford, Russell was intrigued by a female British White Terrier named "Trump". What made Trump unique for a white terrier was that she had dark tan spots over her eyes, ears and tail. Trump was owned by a local milkman whom she accompanied on his daily rounds, door to door. When the young Russell saw the dog in the streets of Oxford on its daily route, he was immediately struck with an idea, and bought her from the milkman on the spot. Russell would soon use Trump as the foundation for his breeding program, breeding her with the standard Fox Terrier of the time in order to create a new, more distinctive coloring pattern, while still retaining the desirable traits already present in the breed.

The original Fox Terrier breed that Russell started with was much different than its modern day counterpart. In the early 1800's the breed was slender and lanky. It was taller, larger and the coloring was predominantly black, tan and reddish brown, very much resembling the fox that it hunted. One of the major issues that Reverend Russell wanted to address is that the dogs were often mistaken for the prey being hunted, and many a time was accidentally shot by their owners when involved in a fast paced chase.

After he completed his studies at Oxford, John Russell was ordained as a minister in 1819 by Dr. Pelham, Bishop of Exeter and one of the clergy favored by King George the Fourth of England himself. He started a family and lived in Swymbridge for a time before settling in Devonshire where he would spend the rest of his days preaching and breeding Fox Terriers. Reverend Russell made careful plans to start a new line of Fox Terrier that would fix the previous problems with the breed by breeding Trump, and later other British White Terriers into the Fox Terrier gene pool. In doing this Russell was careful to only introduce enough of the White Terrier's genetic stock into the Fox Terrier gene pool to differentiate it from a real Fox, but not enough to carry the many defects of the White Terrier breed onto the new Fox Terrier line.

The British White Terrier was known as a lap dog to most dog enthusiasts of England at the time. The breed was completely white in most cases and ranged in size from 10 to 20 lbs. Although stocky and muscular the breed was rarely, if ever, used for any type of work, they were regarded as too small and fragile to be of much use for anything. Also detracting from the breed's popularity was its reputation for being prone to partial or complete deafness, among other deformities caused by in-breeding.

It took several generations of careful breeding, but within twelve years Reverend John Russell had created the ideal form of the Fox Terrier. This new line became wildly popular among hunting enthusiasts and British aristocrats, soon replacing the old black and tan standard of the breed completely.

Although the British White Terrier proved useful for improving the Fox Terrier and several other breeds, the breed itself held very little regard among English society. Thanks to the unpopularity of the White Terrier, the breed was completely extinct by the year 1900. It is important to note however, several of Reverend Russell's experimental breeding lines of Fox Terrier exhibited almost a completely white coloring pattern as well as other British White Terrier traits. Many of those breeding lines still exist today.

Russell often broke the stodgy stereotype of someone in his position; being known as a man who enjoyed good living and fine entertainment. Russell was known for enjoying the company of others and attending social gatherings. The minister also indulged his passion for hunting and sport, which earned him the nickname of "The Sporting Parson". Those close to him had also given him the nickname of "Jack" which is where the name of the breed he would later by synonymous with originates from.

Although John Russell had become extremely popular among the Fox hunting community of Britain, his passion for the breed would cost him dearly in his chosen career. Russell was rarely granted promotions or positions of elevated status in the clergy. Many of his superiors felt that he spent too much time Fox hunting and looked down on his reputation as "The Sporting Parson". One member of the clergy in particular who expressed public disdain for the young Reverend's activities was a Bishop Phillpotts. Phillpott's felt that the idea of a "Sporting Parson" would bring embarrassment and trouble to the church. After many years Russell's friendly nature would eventually win over even the stodgy Bishop's confidence, and the two developed a mutual respect and grudging acquaintance.

Although his love for the breed may have stymied his career in the church, his love for dogs granted him immense pleasures as well as other opportunities within the breeding and showing communities. Russell was well known for traveling over fifty miles on horseback just to arrive at a designated hunting location, and then travel again the fifty miles back in the pitch black of night.

In his lifetime Russell would become one of the original founding members of The Kennel Club, the first ever officially recognized and sanctioned dog breeders and showers association. In 1876 Russell would be the first person to write the officially recognized breed standard for the Fox Terrier as a show dog. This standard has remained relatively unchanged by professional dog showing societies for the last 132 years.

What is interesting to note is that it's said that although Russell would become involved in the organization and judging of dog shows, he would never show any dogs from his own breeding line saying "the difference between my dogs and show dogs can be likened to the difference between wild and cultivated flowers."

In his golden years Russell's reputation had even attracted the attention of Prince Edward, who befriended the aging dog breeder and frequently enjoyed his company. The prince would later go on to become King Edward the Seventh of England.

Although a social darling among the finer citizens of England, Russell had fallen on financial difficulty a number of times throughout his life. Neither Preaching nor Fox Hunting paid particularly well and Russell was regularly forced to sell off large portions of his breeding and hunting stock in order to make ends meet. Over time he would build his pack up again, only to have to sell them off when money got tight. Russell decided to quit breeding the Fox terrier in 1870, but continued to maintain his own pack of hunting dogs and be involved in the organization of dog shows. By 1883 he kept only a small pack of four dogs, all of them aged and non-breeding.

By that time Russell had been involved with Fox Terriers for sixty five years. Russell lived on the homestead he had established for his family decades earlier in Devonshire, England, The property was known as "Black Torring". One day, in the spring of 1883 and for unknown reasons, Russell gathered together all of his sermons, as well as his documents, records, and papers that recorded the history of his work with the Fox Terrier. He brought the documents out to his veranda overlooking the rolling hills of the country side and spread them out on a table in front of him, pouring over the decades of memories. A few hours later, one of his sons would arrive to visit and find hundreds of pages of his father's documents floating freely in the breeze. Pages were scattered throughout the property and along the countryside. On Saturday, May 16th 1883 Reverend John Russell was found by his son deceased of natural causes, still sitting on his veranda with his records spread out before him.

It's safe to say that the Revered had been the world's leading expert on Fox Terriers at the time. Although the family had tried to retrieve his papers, many of the Reverend's documents were lost forever, blown away on the winds. This makes it very difficult to pinpoint many details regarding the early history of the Jack Russell Terrier, especially in regards to breeding lines; the blood line of his original dog "Trump"; and what, if any other breeds of dog aside from the British White Terrier were introduced into his breeding program in order to achieve his results.

The Reverend was quite famous for his fun-loving reputation and expertise in sport hunting at the time of his death. Although somewhat aware of his popularity, even he would have been surprised at the response to his death. Thousands of people mourned the death of "The Sporting Parson", not just in Britain, but the world over. News of the Reverend's Death made its way across much of the civilized world, even making headlines in the New York Times.

A few short years after Reverend Russell's death, representatives of the Kennel Club announced at their annual showing that the name of the Fox Terrier would be officially changed to the Jack Russell Terrier. The Kennel Club felt that this gesture was fitting in order to recognize the important contributions that the beloved Reverend had made. Although the death of Reverend John Russell would be the end of his story, it was far from the end of the story for the Jack Russell Terrier.

At the time of Reverend Russell's death, Fox hunting was still a prominent sport in British society, and the sport continued to play an important and integral part in the history and development of the Jack Russell Terrier. The sport of fox hunting is one type of chase hunting, also known as venery. Venery dates back to ancient Egyptian and

Babylonian times. Ancient Celtics in what would become known as Britain took part in chase hunting, using a breed of dog known as the Agassaei. When the Roman's ruled the land they brought Castorian and Fulpine hounds to Britain, taking part in venery hunts of hare, deer and wild boar.

When William the Conqueror arrived in England he brought the Gascon and the Talbot hound to the region and regularly took part in venery. This is where the fox hunting expression "Tally-Ho!" comes from, a translation of the old French word "Taillis-au!", which signals to the hunting party that the that the game they are searching for has been spotted among the nearby patches of brush.

The first recorded practice of modern fox hunting was in Norfolk, England in 1534. At that time many regions in Britain were over populated with foxes, considered a pest akin to the rat because of their sheer numbers. Frustrated, farmers began to gather with groups of their own hounds and form hunting parties to hunt down and thin out the fox population. These fox hunting posses were formed regularly by rural farmers to help rid each other's lands of the foxes who posed a danger to their livestock. Farmer's herds often suffered from foxes that would attack the smaller or weaker livestock for food, sometimes attack large animals spreading disease, and most commonly have a horse or cow break its leg by stepping into the opening of a foxes den.

Eventually the practice became a regular form of land maintenance, and the thrill of the hunt became a part of rural life. When the nobles of Britain noticed this tradition, it wasn't long before they decided this would be an exciting sport for young men to take part in during their formative years. Eventually the aristocrats would begin holding annual fox hunts in conjunction with other annual social events, and planning new events around a fox hunt. The oldest annual fox hunt event is likely the Bilsdale hunt held in Yorkshire, England. By the late 1600's fox hunting had become so popular that breeders, wealthy citizens, and entrepreneurial farmers were all breeding and training dogs specifically for the use of fox hunting.

The tradition of the fox hunt carried on, but made a significant change in the late 1700's and early 1800's. It is important to note that by this time Fox hunting had become so popular among the upper crust of society that it was considered a sign of status and social standing. The wealthy found it easier to partake in fox hunting regularly because they had more leisure time and could afford to own an entire pack of hunting dogs to use whenever they wanted. This contrasted greatly with the farmers who first created the practice, who would have to call together a large number of neighbors in order to arrange a hunt.

It was at this time that the British government passed a number of legal acts which required rural residents to erect fences and other barriers between their properties in order to help prevent land disputes. This meant that hunting parties could no longer pass from field to field without being blocked off by barricades. Soon hunting enthusiasts incorporated this challenge into the regular practice of fox hunting by expecting these barricades and training their horses to jump the obstacles with long strides, losing very little ground during the chase. It was this ingenuity which led to today's modern horse jumping sport, and is also the reason why many dog competitions include small fence jumping events for Jack Russell's.

By the 1800's the modern fox hunting pack as we know it today was common. Unlike the movies, which often portray a person hunting fox with an entire pack of

Bloodhounds or sometimes just one Beagle or Basset Hound, a real fox hunting pack consists of several different breeds. Professional hunters will often be accompanied by a pack of ten or more dogs. This pack would include several Foxhounds, Beagles and Jack Russell Terriers. Some hunters will even use the odd Dachshund or Greyhound for different purposes.

Each and every breed included in a fox hunting pack is included for a different and specific purpose. Foxhounds are used for their incredible sense of smell and ability to lead the party onto the right scent trail to begin the hunt. Beagles are used for their deep, loud, bellowing howl alerting the rest of the hunting party to their location should they find an animal, or get too far ahead of the pack. The Jack Russell plays one of the most important parts of the hunt. It is often the strength and courage of the Jack Russell that is needed in order to bring the hunt to a close. A frightened fox will often hide in the nearest available burrow, far below where the rest of the hunting party can reach. Without hesitation the Jack Russell will use its smaller size to crawl right in after its prey, often either scaring the fox out of an adjoining tunnel, or killing it underground and dragging it back up to the light of day. The Jack Russell continued to flourish with the popularity of the fox hunt and quickly became one of the most desired breeds in Britain.

The first major change to the world of the Jack Russell came in the World War II era. By this time, much of the world was wrapped up in the new and developing war effort. Citizens had little time for fox hunting. Especially with the men going off to battle, there was very little demand for any type of working dog unless it could be used to help soldiers in the front line. This left many breeds of working dogs without anyone interested in breeding them or ensuring their survival throughout the war time. Luckily for the Jack Russell, its disposition and popularity had endeared it to the public and it was one of the few lucky work dog breeds that were embraced into the common English home, making the transition from field hand to household pet. Following the conclusion of World War II, England experienced resurgence in the popularity of sport hunting. This also led to resurgence in the Jack Russell's popularity. Soon Jack Russell's were once again seen scouring the fields of England with hunting parties and tunneling into fox dens.

In the late forties and early fifties, breeders once again discovered the Jack Russell. A number of breeders took it upon themselves to improve the breed further. Intensive breeding programs selected dogs with only the most specific attributes to create a new line of Jack Russell that was shorter, stockier, and more muscled than previous generations. This new compact model of the Jack Russell would eventually become the most commonly found version of the breed. Some have claimed that a number of popular breeders had introduced stock from other breeds such as the Bull Terrier in order to achieve their results. Those claims have never been substantiated with any sort of documentation.

On the tail end of the new boom in fox hunting came a resurgence in another type of dog event. Although dog shows had been popular in British society for nearly two hundred years at that point, a new generation of enthusiast and Kennel Club members took the dog show a step further, propelling the popularity of such events into mainstream British society.

The Jack Russell has always been an animal that was out of place when it came to shows of appearance and strict manners. Most breeders of fine hunting Terriers and hunting enthusiasts themselves had no interest in the standard dog show and no inclination toward parading their Jack Russell around a ring in order to be judged on appearance and style alone. On the other hand a new generation of Jack Russell owners who were now used to the breed being embraced in the home had no desire to bring their pets out into the field; however they were very enthusiastic about showcasing their little darling for the public as a part the new national phenomenon. The one thing that the two sides could agree on was that a Jack Russell was not a dog you could judge on appearance and manners, but one that could only be proven by tests of skill and endurance.

Although most Jack Russell breeders and owners were not interested in shows, and therefore had nothing to do with them, the few Jack Russell's that were entered into dog shows became a popular feature and continue to be to this day. In the instances when Jack Russell's do appear in dog shows and skill trials; rarely are they judged on appearance and form, and more on their ability to jump, race, retrieve, crawl in tunnels and overcome obstacles. It should be noted however that there is indeed a specified appearance standard for the Jack Russell in place with the Kennel Club, the American Kennel Club, Jack Russell Terrier Club of America, and most other dog shows and organizations. Jack Russell Terriers who do not meet these requirements are often still allowed to compete in skills events, but are barred from participating in any dog showing events. The new heyday that the Jack Russell was enjoying would soon fall down around its ears.

In the late sixties and early seventies, the free love movement also brought along with it a number of new animal rights groups that protested the inhumane treatment of animals. These groups set their sights firmly on the practice of fox hunting; targeting it as cruel and inhumane to the fox, and also raising issues about the ethical treatment of the dogs used in the hunt as well. The main point of contention was that many hunters considered a dog to be beyond its usefulness once it was beyond five years old. Many hunters would put down healthy dogs, based solely on their age and the possibility of having outlived their usefulness. Public outcry against the practice of fox hunting quickly resulted in the popularity of the sport to decline. Critics declared publicly that the sport was barbaric and uncivilized; causing it to fall out of fashion with many of Britain's elite and wealthy. The sudden drop in the popularity of the very sport that Jack Russell's were famous for meant that a number of trainers and breeding operations went out of business. The number of Jack Russell's being born every year plummeted and their total numbers hit an all-time low, endangering the beloved breed.

The sport of fox hunting did survive, and the Jack Russell continued to be bred by remaining fox hunting enthusiasts, the fox hunting industry as a whole is just much smaller than it once was. With the drop of popularity in sports considered to be "uncivilized", a renewed interest arose in hobbies and activities that were considered acceptable. One such hobby that experienced a new surge in interest was dog showing. As previously mentioned, the Jack Russell Terrier has always had a strange relationship with the dog show. Most Jack Russell owners have resisted any sort of grading of their animals based on their appearance, mostly because the value many owners find in the breed is not in their looks, but their working and problem solving skills. It is for this reason that most organized events for Jack Russell's consist of field trials and jumping exercises.

There are showing events that do allow Jack Russell's and there is a portion of Jack Russell owners who take part in such events. The majority of Jack Russell's do not meet the appearance requirements for showing, and those that do are rarely ever trained to work the field and perform complex tasks, but instead trained in obedience and poise for showing. This means that in the majority of cases a Jack Russell is either a show dog or a field dog, not both. Many spectators find the compact size and comical personalities of these feisty little terriers to be the highlight of any organized dog event.

The popularity of dog themed events also gave rise to further interest in these animals, and the Jack Russell once again experienced a resurgence of interest as a family pet in the late seventies and early eighties. New breeders began to establish themselves and build breeding pools based on the Jack Russell not as a working dog or a show dog, but a family pet. Families all over the U.K. and North America began to invite this energy packed dynamo in their home. The energy and intelligence of the Jack Russell has endeared it onto the public, a fondness that has continued to this day.

At some point someone in Hollywood took notice of the energy of the Jack Russell and its ability to learn complex tasks and remain constantly alert. Soon special trainers were teaching these dogs how to act and be involved with movie production. The Jack Russell became famous all over the world as people would watch their antics in movies and on television from the comfort of their own living rooms. Jack Russell's can be observed in television shows such as Fraser, Wishbone, Chef Rick Stein, television commercials and more. Movies in recent history that have featured the Jack Russell have been The Mask starring Jim Carrey, Crimson Tide, The Earnest movies, Harry Potter and many more. The increasing presence of the Jack Russell in film and media has made it one of the most desirable breeds of dog known today.

Because in most cases Kennel Club Jack Russell's, or those bred for show, are not bred with those that work the field or live as family pets, the breed itself has begun to develop specific distinctions between each branch of its family tree. These differences have now begun to be regarded as signs of two separate, but related official breeds. The Jack Russell or Fox Terriers being used for dog showing events have developed a larger chest and longer head, among several other differences in body structure. The division between show and pet breeders has led to a new division in the breed, with the show breed now being officially recognized as the Parson Russell Terrier.

The Parson Russell is the result of the same original genetic stock as the Jack Russell Terrier, but due to selective breeding and genetic adapting to their new use as a show dog, the offshoot breed has developed its own unique characteristics. Those characteristics include the aforementioned longer head and large chest, but also include an overall slightly larger body size and more subdued personality. Parson Russell's are still energetic just like their Jack Russell Cousins, but seem to be more obedient, likely due to the dog showing environment that they have been trained to work in. The Parson Russell Terrier was first recognized as an official breed in the UK in 1990 and in North America in 2001.

Because of this new distinction it is now most common to see only Parson Russell Terriers in showing events, and Jack Russell Terriers in sporting and field events. Today enthusiasts of each individual breed tend to focus on the types of events that their breed is known for and rarely cross over into the other or do both. The Parson Russell Terrier is not the first offshoot or variation in the Jack Russell breed. Thanks to the various breeding lines dating back to Reverend Russell himself, as well as the breeders who experimented further with the breed's appearance in the 1950's, a number of different lines with different characteristics have been established.

There are wire haired Jack Russell's, with rough coats as long at ten centimeters. Smooth haired Jack Russell's with a very short layer of smooth fur. The broken coated Jack Russell's have a coat that is a combination of both smooth and rough fur. Long-Legged Jack Russell's resemble their shorter counterparts, but have a leg length that is several inches higher. Various combinations of those traits appear in many lines as well, and some litters can consist of Jack pups that exhibit traits from any of those different variations. These variations in Jack Russell appearance, such as rough and smooth furred versions, are believed to be the result of selective breeding of various lines within the species. Some believe that the differences may be attributed to the introduction of other breeds into the gene pool, but no one has ever been able to substantiate the claims. This speculation has led many to refer to the Jack Russell as "the most popular mutt in the world."

It has been speculated that the variations may originate from Reverend John Russell's original breeding pool, and the possibility that he introduced other breeds in order to achieve certain qualities, as he did with the British White Terrier.

Are there other breeds in the history of the Jack Russell's genetics? Because of the loss of much of Reverend Russell's valuable documents it is a mystery that we will likely never know the answer to. It's safe to say that in the last 178 years of the Jack Russell Terrier's existence the small, but mighty breed has left an indelible mark upon the face of history. This mark includes significant contributions to culture, sport, entertainment and family living. Although endangered on more than one occasion the Jack Russell has proven that it's feisty nature, tons of energy and fearless attitude will continue to ensure its survival and continue to play a part in shaping modern society for a long time to come.

Chapter 2

The Personality and Temperament of the Jack Russell Terrier

It's important to note that above all, the Jack Russell Terrier is a working Terrier, a breed of dog specifically bred to perform specific tasks. The entire reason for the Jack Russell's existence is to run, hunt, chase and flush out fox and other animals. They were specifically breed to perform this task aggressively throughout England. It's the excitement and rush of the hunt that can be credited for the infamous personality and temperament of the Jack Russell.

Part of this breeding has ingrained a very vocal personality and penchant for barking in the breed. This is not a "nuisance" but a desirable trait that is supposed to be represented in the breed in order to do the job it was designed for. The reason that a vocal nature is necessary in the Jack Russell is so that hunters could find the dog during the excitement of the hunt. The Jack Russell quite routinely was placed at the front of the pack and was meant to run far ahead of the other hounds and hunters.

While in pursuit of its prey the Jack Russell is rarely concerned about the location of its owner and can often find himself well beyond viewing range of the hunt party. If a Jack Russell were to chase the game away and not communicate with a series of loud barks, not only would the hunting party not know where the dog is, but they wouldn't know where the dog had located its prey at; they would have no idea in which way to go or where to find their game.

Another reason that vocalism makes the Jack valuable is that they will often follow prey into their burrows and tunnel after them underground. If the dog is already underground the only way to know the location of the dog is to follow the sound of its bark coming from beneath the soil. Jacks sometimes find themselves stuck in these tunnels, which is why every good hunter brings a shovel with him in order to dig the Jack out if the need arises. The bark can often let the hunter know where to dig in order to get close, and where not to dig, so the dog isn't injured by the shovel. This is why the Jack Russell was bred to be very vocal, and why even non-hunting Jack Russell's today exhibit this trait.

The Jack Russell Terrier has also been bred to be very intelligent. The nature of the work that Jack Russell's are meant for is unpredictable at best. There is rarely a consistent hunting experience unless a hunter chooses to hunt the same spot every time of a regular basis. This is rare. Even if the same location is used consistently, there are often obstacles that haven't been encountered on previous hunts. The most valuable Jack Russell's are the ones who can meet challenges and do complex problem solving on the spot in order to gain the advantage. Much of the prey hunted by the Jack Russell, such as the fox and the raccoon are equally as intelligent and it takes a clever dog in order outsmart the sly and elusive game it is hunting.

Many dog lovers have gravitated towards the breed for its friendly, curious personality and diminutive size. Although a popular pet and excellent companion, it pays to do your research the Jack Russell and know what want and what to expect from them. There is a misconception among the general public thanks to movies and TV that the Jack Russell is a quiet helper and lap dog that will relax with you after a long day. The traits and characteristics are something that has been purposely created and highly desirable to the generations of breeders who have cared for the Jack Russell. Above all they prize this dog for being fearless, intelligent and alert. A dog that is truly ready to face the world head-on without a second thought. If you use a Jack Russell as a lap dog you will end up with a very unhappy dog that will likely destroy your house.

The dog portrayed in films is an example of a highly trained professional working dog that has been trained to behave a certain way on camera. He is an actor. This depiction does not in any way represent the behavior of the real life Jack Russell in a family setting. Just because the dog is small does not make it a lap dog. He may enjoy lying on your lap from time to time, when the mood strikes him, but that will only be a very small percentage of the time.

Jack Russell's are best suited to a home with an active family who enjoy the outdoors. Jack Russell's will do best in a rural or country setting where there is wilderness for them to run, explore and play in. Keeping your Jack Russell as a welcome part of the family means firm, consistent training and patience. Another key to enjoying your Jack is regular lengthy exercise and fun games to occupy them. Failure to keep your Jack Russell active will often result in a bored dog that will show a change in temperament and quickly find himself in trouble. Your wardrobe, shoes, furniture and other belongings will suffer.

Jack Russell's are very playful and have very flamboyant personalities. Allowing them a chance to exercise these traits will help keep your Jack happy and healthy. Jack Russell's that are not shown the proper care, training and exercise can quickly become an unmanageable member of the family. Jack's that are not properly attended to will often exhibit excessive and unwarranted barking, an unstoppable urge to escape from your home or property, unwanted digging and damage outside and inside the home as well as damage to personal belongings within the home that are within reach.

In the U.S., Canada, and Britain there are now a number of rescue agencies that focus exclusively on Jack Russell's. This is because of the number of people who take these animals into their homes expecting them to be like the dogs on TV. These rescue agencies are often working full time at full capacity to take care of Jack's that have been rejected by their owners. It cannot be expressed enough that anyone interested in Jack Russell Terrier's must do their research and realistically decide if a dog of this type will be able to fit into their current lifestyle before buying or adopting a Jack Russell.

A young Jack Russell may be leery of small children and babies the first time that they encounter them, but will quickly adapt. Once a Jack Russell has become accustomed to the presence of little people he will often enjoy their company and the enthusiasm that children usually show in playing games of fetch and other activities that Jacks love. It's important to note that a Jack Russell will not tolerate being manhandled or abused by anyone, small children or adults. The Jack is unique in this way as it has one of the most well defined senses of personal boundaries of any dog breed, which is often unexpected because of its size. A Jack will quickly and aggressively defend itself against any form of abuse, even unintentional. Very small children who are prone to pinching, grabbing or squeezing the dog should be kept at a safe distance. Children should be taught from an early age how to properly treat the dog and what type of interaction is inappropriate.

Jack Russell's are very friendly and outgoing to both humans and other dogs, often ready to play with other canine breeds upon first meeting. It is very common though for a Jack Russell to exhibit aggression and dominance toward other dogs of the same sex. The male Jack is happy to play with other dogs, as long as they know he is the alpha male. A very common mental quirk among Jack Russell's is what's known as the Napoleon Complex. The Napoleon Complex can best be described as the inability to recognize the reality of a situation. The key trait of this complex is that the dog will behave as if it is much bigger than it is, and refuse to accept any type of dominant behavior from another breed, even if much, much larger. Jack's who exhibit this trait are essentially fearless and will try to press its own dominance onto another animal, no matter its size. It's as if the jack doesn't realize how small it is at all. Their alpha attitude quite surprisingly can work to their advantage, and the Jack has been known to easily scare of dogs and other animals that are much larger than it.

However brave your dog is, you can't always expect luck to work out in his favor if he is a little Napoleon. As often as he is top dog he can also get into situations where a larger dog will respond with extreme aggression, putting your Jack in real danger. It pays to closely supervise your Jack Russell when in the presence of other dogs. These

Napoleon/Jack's often think they are as big as a full grown German Shepherd or Mastiff. It's likely a very good thing that they are not, a Jack Russell of that size would likely terrorize an entire neighborhood.

Egotistical and full of life seems to be one accurate description of the Jack Russell. A Napoleonic Jack will often exhibit territorial issues. They will often mark every inch of their property daily and take the protection of that territory very seriously. When another dog, no matter the size, approaches this Jack's territory he will immediately respond with a growl. When defending territory the Napoleonic Jack will also exhibit bristled hair along his back that will stand up straight and resemble a Mohawk; the tail will point straight up in the air; his head will lower, and his gaze will fix in a menacing glare at the intruder. The Jack will them begin marching forward, eyeing up the violator for a good spot to bite.

Very large breeds will often be shocked by this response and double take as if bewildered. The Jack often uses this state of surprise to further puff up and intimidate the intruder, often scaring off much larger dogs that would normally be more dominant. Some large breeds will be so surprised they will become submissive or flee for their lives in uncertainty. This is just another trademark of your fearless Jack Russell. If your yard is unfenced it is recommended to never leave your Jack out untied or unsupervised. Some dogs won't care how tough your Jack is.

Whether he is of the Napoleonic persuasion or not, your fearless Jack trying to dominate a large aggressive dog may land your little dynamo in some very serious, even fatal danger. Whether you are thinking about or already own a Jack it is wise to inform yourself and carefully consider all of the information available to you. As one expert has put it, just remember…he is Napoleon and YOU are Admiral Nelson. After taking all this Jack Russell Terrier information under consideration, and you know this is just the dog for you, there may be a little Napoleon waiting to make you a very, very proud owner.

If there's one personality complex that the Jack Russell does not suffer from, it would be low self-esteem. Jack Russell's are often confident in themselves to the point of ridiculousness. It's quite common for an adult Jack to display aggression towards cats as well. Because of their history Jack's usually recognize cats as prey that they are meant to chase and hunt down. Given the opportunity a Jack that is not used to cats will quickly chase down and kill it. It's not advised to bring an adult Jack who is not used to cats into a home with cats or any other fur bearing pets or animals. Things like gerbils, hamsters and guinea pigs should be kept well out of site. No matter how safe it is; if a Jack Russell can see it, he will eventually figure out how to get it. Jack Russell's can learn to accept cats and live with them peacefully, but this usually has to be done by raising them from a puppy in a home with a dominant adult cat that will put the dog in his place and remind him of the household pecking order.

The comical personalities and curiosities of the Jack Russell can quickly designate them as the family clown. The energy that the dog possesses makes it always eager to entertain and take part in any active physical activity. The Jack Russell seems to never run out of new ways to amuse. Jack Russell's have been known to play for hours, until they collapse from exhaustion. With a little experimentation, the Jack Russell owner will find that their Jack is just as happy to chase a toy across the living room as it is chasing a fox in the field. They will be as happy to kill a funky old sock under the couch as killing a squirrel in the shed. The key is to keep them active. The Jack Russell does indeed have an intelligent, energetic, assertive personality that makes if an endearing character in any home.

The Jack Russell is also unwaveringly loyal. The mighty little wonder will go to any lengths to protect its home and family. A jack will not hesitate to protect owners and children in its family. Some Jacks have even been known to protect other pets in the family from harm. If a Jack perceives a member of the family to be in danger they will even often protect them by placing their own body between whomever they are protecting and the perceived danger. This loyalty makes the Jack Russell one of the bravest little dog breeds in the world, and many a Jack has been injured or even killed while protecting loved ones from harm.

Thanks to its energy level this mighty little bundle of fur requires a huge investment of time and attention. In order to maintain any sanity in their home life, owners have to focus on activity, exercise, training and discipline. Owners of Jack Russell's also have to exhibit a certain amount of acceptance of their Jack Russell and the history behind the breed that makes him who he is. The owner has to understand the hunting nature that has been bred into the dog and find ways to work with it. Your Jack Russell is who he is, and you will not change him.

In the very early years a Jack Russell must have consistent training and vigorous exercise. Without that ground work in place a Jack Russell can become aggressive, unmanageable, disobey commands, bark excessively, chase strangers, and even exhibit aggression towards guests in your home. A well trained Jack is more than happy to comply with the rules of the home and obey commands…unless they've caught onto the scent of another animal.

It's always advisable to keep your Jack Russell on a leash when out in the public or in wilderness areas you are unfamiliar with. If the dog is loose and catches an interesting scent he will be gone. Jack Russell's seem to suffer from an indefinable, genetic form of deafness, known to people as selective hearing. They appear to hear very well any other time, but when they've caught an interesting scent all your cries of "stop!" and "come back here!" seem to go unheard. It's wise to keep your Jack on a leash in public parks. Jack Russell's don't only see foxes, cats, raccoons and other furry animals as an enemy. Jack Russell's have also been known to aggressively attack, defend against, and hunt any digging or crawling animal, even snakes.

As previously stated, Jack Russell's do not possess the fears that humans do. A Jack Russell will respond to an aggressive snake in the same way as an aggressive dog, and even chase them to their holes and dig if need be to catch them. Many Jack Russell's have met an untimely end from a poisonous snake. It's recommended to never leave your dog unattended in a place where it may encounter such an animal. If possible it's best to avoid any type of snake altogether. Although a Jack Russell can and will easily kill snakes, poisonous or not; non-poisonous snakes can still present a danger. Some species of non-poisonous snakes will have long, hooked fangs and will bite your dog in self defense. If these bites become infected they are not treatable on the surface because the infection is actually nowhere near the puncture wound. These types of infected wounds can result in fatal blood poisoning or painful and expensive surgery. It is best to simply avoid snakes altogether.

When bringing animals together it's important not to leave them unattended for any length of time, especially if there are more than two Jacks. Jacks have a pack hunting mentality, a natural instinct from hundreds of years of breeding. They will exhibit those traits. It's very unwise to leave two or more jacks alone with a cat or another pet. A Jack that has previously been non-aggressive towards cats and other animals may take part in the killing of such an animal when in the pack environment. There have even been cases where some Jacks have ganged up on a weaker one in the pack and injured or even killed it. A close eye on the dynamic of any pet gathering involving the Jack Russell is advisable. Again, it is possible that this can happen no matter how cute or well trained your dog is. It's in their nature, the behavior is instinctual and no amount of training will overpower the animal's instincts entirely.

First time owners will often find they are overwhelmed and wonder why the dog's needs are so demanding. It's best to know what you are getting into before hand and make sure that your home has the time and environment to meet those needs before bringing a Jack Russell home. Although the Jack Russell owner always has to be alert of the potential dangers, many owners will eventually come to think of their Jack as more of a person than a dog. The unique and intelligent personalities exhibited find many owners considering their Jacks to be like a child. Owners will even find themselves worried about their Jack's mood and happiness. This is because the Jack is prone to mood swings.

A Jack who hasn't been allowed to run outside recently will often mope and appear to have "the blues". Jack's involved in an excited and energetic home will also find themselves becoming hyper to the point of being irritating. As rare as it is, a dog as excitable as the Jack will even find himself feeling lazy from time to time and decide to stretch out next to the fireplace for a nap. At times a frustrated Jack can even exhibit a preference for independence, even rebellion. It's all a part of a rich, exhausting tapestry. With these things in mind, it's easy to see why the proper environment is important to maintain the famous traits of the Jack Russell temperament.

They need to run. They need to hunt. They need to play. And in down times, they need to be shown intimate affection. When enjoying downtime Jack Russell's love to snuggle. They enjoy nothing more than making you keep them warm in your own bed, and taking up as much space as possible while doing it. If a Jack Russell is in the mood for petting and isn't getting, it will let you know by forcefully ramming its head under your hand and making it run along his head. It's best to take the hint and give him some affection.

A prime example of the change in mood is the sudden switch that a Jack Russell can make from being your lovable cutie to a snarling beast when encountering a dangerous animal. This trait was highly desired by the hunters who created the breed, and necessary for them to do their job. It's this sudden toughness that has made them able to combat and defeat even the meanest fox in his own home.

The main point of focus that any researcher should take away with them is that although the descriptions of the Jack Russell personality may seem to contradict each other, in fact is signifies the duality in the breeds personality that is necessary for it to function as both a loyal companion and a fearless hunter. The Jack Russell is as dominant as a French dictator and as lovable as Lassie, that's just how it is. Many Jack Russell owners have learned to accept this personality and wouldn't have their beloved companion any other way. The assertiveness, the drama, the fearlessness, the arrogance and the loyalty are all a part of the Jack Russell experience, wrapped up in a muscular little bundle. The Jack Russell has a style of personality that many dog enthusiasts have come to admire. Good Jack Russell owners usually find it fairly easy to accept their Jack Russell's personalities because in the end, even with all of his quirks, there is a bond of unconditional love between the dog and its owner.

Managing and Promoting Good Behavior

Again, owners have to understand and have a certain level of acceptance for the behavior of their pet, without allowing him to run wild and become a danger or a nuisance to others. Just remember that the Jack Russell is supposed to be the most stubborn, strong willed, defiant breed on the planet. It's highly cautioned that you do not attempt to use corporal punishment to correct your Jack's behavior. Aside from possibly creating aggressiveness issues towards people, it just won't work. You may be able to give him a slap once or twice, but that will be it. He's not stupid. Why would he come to you just to get hit? This type of punishment usually causes more problems than solutions, as the Jack will likely not come to you when you want him to in the future for training and commands.

Jacks are highly intelligent and not likely to give themselves up for abuse. Jack's often know when they've done wrong and will expect scolding, even exhibiting submission behavior before you know what they've done. Using physical punishment will mean that you can kiss any sense of remorse in your Jack Russell goodbye. They'll be gone before you can get anywhere near them. They're fast too. They were bred to chase fox, which is a very swift animal. Stop chasing them; you're not going to catch them. The best way to train a Jack is to vocally scold them for bad behavior, and possibly include a short time out in a restricted area. Many people advise against using the crate as a time-out zone because it may make the dog unwilling to go into the crate, which you want him to feel safe and comfortable in, not punished.

The best results come from reinforcing good behavior with a combination of treats and clicker training. Jack Russell's do have a good memory and will remember what they like and don't like. You usually can't fool them with the same trick more than twice, and it doesn't take long for them to figure out how to get what they want and avoid what they don't. One famous story tells of a man whose Jack Russell would wake up promptly at 1:30 am and begin to bark incessantly for no apparent reason. The man finally came up with a plan. He devised a system of ropes and pulleys tied to a bucket placed over the dog's kennel that filled from a garden hose. The end of the rope was tied to the man's nightstand next to his bed. That night when the dog began barking, the man pulled the rope, causing the bucket to tip and douse the dog with water. The man did this every time the dog would begin barking unnecessarily. After two nights of this the dog quit barking in the middle of the night and never did it again. While this story may have been embellished over time, and seem a little extreme for most owners, it does illustrate the characteristics of the Jack Russell to "learn from its mistakes".

Trying to stop barking from extreme territorialism can be quite more challenging than that little story. Especially when you consider that barking is a quite natural reaction for the Jack Russell because of its breeding history. In the past the Jack Russell was supposed to view all of its surroundings as its territory and bark as an alarm when other people or animals were in it. The best way to practice good ownership and good neighbor relations is to prevent any unnecessary barking behavior before it starts. The way to do this is to start from an early age, as soon as you bring your puppy home. The dog is smart and will learn from repetition. The key to success is consistency. Scold negative behavior and reward good behavior or responding to the command when you say "no" or "stop".

The most important detail in order to successfully train your Jack is to evaluate what is acceptable consistency. Do it every time and do it immediately. Scold bad behavior, reward good, do it every time, and your Jack will be much more manageable as an adult. During the early training period it is best that the Jack Russell pup be kept indoors while the owner is away instead of in a fenced yard; unless another care provider will be present in order to administer the same strict correction as the owner in their absence. Remember, it's very much discouraged to try and achieve success in training by physically harming the dog or breaking its spirit. The jack Russell's behavior is rooted in its ancestry and breeding, using violence to correct it will often create more personality problems in this strong willed breed. A well trained Jack Russell will enjoy pleasing its master and spending time with them. A happy Jack will exhibit more loyalty and affection than the owner can handle. Remember to be understanding, no Jack, even the best trained will respond perfectly to every command 100% of the time.

Chapter 3

The Training of Jack Russell Terriers

In the dog world, aggression is a very dirty word. This is something that many dog owners, even professional breeders not only come into contact with, but conflict on. In a nutshell most forms of aggression are one of the most natural traits and instincts that have been bred into your dog, and they will occur, its nature. However, this same instinct has been used as an excuse to surrender, abandon even euthanize, thousands of dogs if not more. Dogs have existed for thousands of years with their only tools of communication between each other to be biting and growling. Many inexperienced individuals often see this as aggression in the wrong situation. Dogs communicate to each other through body language. This often consists of growling as well as physical contact which includes mouthing and use of teeth. Bringing a dog into your home with the expectations of efficient training and the complete elimination of all forms of aggressive communication is almost as absurd as asking a person to become deaf and blind at will.

Over the centuries dog owners have bred into dogs the instincts of loyalty, companionship, and the enjoyment of being petted, touched, or even snuggling with humans. This is not a natural condition for any species of animal, but has been collectively imprinted upon the dog psyche and passed along from their ancestors. Of course being the descendant of a sociable dog doesn't mean that a dog will be equally sociable. Any dog must have firm training, supervisions and discipline in order to be compatible with any human family.

It wasn't too long ago, just a few hundred years really, that most breeds of dog would have lived in the wilderness, roamed wild, had no interest in humans, and enjoyed nothing more than chasing down and ripping apart any prey to be found. No matter what methods we use to train, those instincts will always and forever be a part of the mental make-up of your dog. Many breeds have adapted this behavior to physical play and rough housing with other dogs, playing with owners, and hunting chew toys. This type of activity is a much needed outlet for any dog, especially a Jack Russell in order to release pent up energy and stress. These dogs have adapted those hunter/killer instincts into something to do for fun without anyone getting hurt (most of the time). This "fun" is necessary for many breeds, especially the Jack Russell, in order to cope with the change in lifestyle and living conditions that their ancestors enjoyed. When you bring a Jack Russell into a home that demands no physical interaction, excitement, rough housing and above all physical communication, you are taking away the one tool that they have in order to deal with their unnatural surroundings; the lifestyle of being an obedient pet as opposed to a wild carnivorous beast.

This is why physical outdoor activity is so important for a Jack Russell. The reason that he has hunted your home and ripped apart your leather jacket is because you aren't giving him an outlet to expend his natural aggression. To him even the destruction of a sandal is a small victory and a successful hunt. When the dog is punished and scolded for this behavior they don't understand what it is that they have done to incur your wrath. Until you had become irate with them, they were proud of their accomplishment and believed they had done a good thing.

Now you've brought this little savage beast into your home and suddenly everything is off-limits, also there's no communication between them and any other animal or person. Your home environment appears be the same as any other number of places they've ever been, but for some reason they're not allowed to do or be anything other than a statue that used to be a dog. Scolding a dog for their natural behavior will only confuse them and creates an environment where the dog may be very unhappy. Once used to your home a Jack considers you to be a part of his pack. Whether or not he thinks he's the head of the pack is another story. A properly trained Jack should be able to have some fun and still recognize that you are the alpha leader. Even when he does recognize you as the boss, he still doesn't understand why he can't play with you the way he would with any other member of his pack.

Denying your dog to behave in any form that is natural to a dog will only create more confusion and frustration. The frustration will grow and eventually the positive aggression traits that were previously shown, (and you've trained out of him) will develop into negative aggression in terms of being cross or frustrated with the people and places surrounding them. In his heart your dog wants to escape. This is when your dog may become a danger to you as well as other people or pets in the household. He will begin to see them as barriers to his own freedom and his ability to interact and communicate with the world around him.

There are a number of things that can be done in order to prevent your Jack Russell Terrier form becoming a negatively aggressive danger to you and the people in your home. The biggest item to do is lower your expectations. The dog is not going to be perpetually silent, sit perfectly straight and upright in a chair and have afternoon tea with you. He's a dog, let him be a dog. One of the biggest causes of grief for owners is trying to impose some type of human standard of manners onto your dog.

Your dog is going to chew. If he's a puppy he will begin teething and chew even more. If he has nothing to chew on other than your $900 Italian shoes, well, that was your fault. In order to allow your dog to explore its natural behavior and still save your home and belongings; you need to use proper training in a patient, firm and consistent manner.

Provide objects that you dog can chew on and remind him what is appropriate for him to chew on and what is not. Be sure that you are the one consistently providing the approved chewing devices and giving the frequent reminders. An important point in training often over looked by the average pet owner is to train him not to chew or mouth human skin. This type of conditioning can prevent a potentially serious injury in extreme circumstances later on down the road.

Tips on Properly Conditioning Your Dog and Setting the Right Environment
- Allow him to mouth, chew, and yes even destroy his toys. That is the reason dog toys were created. If you don't like spending money on them you should have considered that factor before getting a dog. If you are still worried about the expense, buy cheaper toys. He will kill these toys that are why it's fun.
- Allow him to mouth cold, wet, or frozen towels. Especially in the teething stages.
- Allow him to mouth his canine playmates. Remember that mouthing is okay, biting is different. Mouthing should not hurt the other animal, should not draw blood, and should not be done by your dog in a way in which he appears angry or snarling.

When he mouths things that are unacceptable there are different methods you can try such as spraying bitter apple or dishwashing soap mixed with water onto the objects he is chewing (and also on your arms and hands, if he is mouthing you). He's not stupid, if it tastes bad and he learns that it consistently tastes bad, soon he'll have no desire to have it in his mouth. Provide a substitute activity such as handing him a chew toy that he may mouth and then playing with him. Playtime should be used as a reward for mouthing and chewing the appropriate items.

If your dog communicates with you by growling in your presence you may need to work on building up trust with the animal. Teach him by showing that nothing bad happens when you gently roll him on his back. As a matter of fact, when he rolls on his back, give him little pieces of dried liver treats or small dog biscuits. Act happy and pleasant when he behaves appropriately with you. When he growls scrunch up your face and snarl. Dogs read our bodies much better than they understand our words.

You can teach the dog that he can trust you by teaching a "leave it" command and then releasing him from the "leave it" with an "OK!" Do this by taking a toy or special treat and telling him "leave it". Gently insist that he not sniff or lick the item. Reward him verbally for when he looks away from it; GOOD DOG! Then tell him "OK!" and let him have it. This way he learns patience, respect for you, and trust!

In aggression prevention it's important to establish proper communication with your dog. Construct a relationship with him that's built on love, trust and mutual respect. Your Jack Russell does not intuitively know that he can trust you. This is something he will learn and something you must earn. You earn your dog's trust by being honest. Don't wave a treat in front of his face and then not feed it to him. Don't call saying, "cookie" and then not deliver on the promised goods.

Build trust by teaching your dog that anything you might do to him is OK and will not hurt him. Couple undesirable occurrences, like a vet visit, with lots of positive reinforcement. Next time you take your pet to the vet, stop by the park on the way home. Feed him a treat after the injections, and praise and reassure him while the vet is examining him. Be sure to reward only confident behavior. If your pet cowers or turns into a wimp don't say or do anything. Either of these could be misunderstood as praise or acceptance of the cowardly behavior. Cowardly behavior can lead to fear. Fear leads to aggression. The next rung of the ladder is fear biting.

If you fire him up, help him cool down. What we view as aggression can be brought on by many common occurrences in a dog's life. Consider, for example, the high adrenaline activities Terriers enjoy; racing, go-to-ground, agility, bike riding, and Frisbee. Even as puppies, we fire them up and send them into the earth. When Terriers go-to ground we pull our dog out of his safe crate into an unfamiliar environment, lead him over to this dark hole, fire him up and "boom" like lightening he's off to find the rats or whatever other monsters might inhabit the earth. Your dog is having a grand time. This is his element! He is home! All his primal instincts kick in. The adrenaline is pumping, his hearts racing, and he's ready to kill. He gets to the caged rats and his little body explodes with barking and snarling. The killing machine is armed and dangerous.

Yes, your little love machine whom loves to cuddle and get rubbed behind his ears is now dangerous. He's a loaded gun. What happens next is really tough on your dog. You come and drag him away from the very prey he was going to have fun killing. If you drag him over to a crate and shove him in it makes things even worse. Your pet has not cooled down. He is still wired, and now he's trapped in the crate. The emotional roller coaster is intense. He will most likely whine, howl, moan and cause a ruckus. It's because he feels like someone who's been wrongfully imprisoned and doesn't know why.

Your dog has gone from being crated in an unfamiliar place, which is only moderately exciting, to being completely fired up, ready for the kill. Then he's smashed back into the crate, waiting. Now what? Nothing happens. Nobody comes back for him. He's stuck in his crate with nothing to do and his adrenaline exploding. Now he can hear that other dogs are being given a shot at killing those rats that he was taken from. The adrenaline is not settling. He doesn't understand that this is a game. He has not learned to enjoy it. Your dog is frustrated and confused.

How to make your dog less frustrated and confused
- Take him to several practice meets before entering him in a trial. Make sure you praise him a lot for leaving the rats and give him something special (like a piece of hot dog, favorite rawhide, or a bear hug.
- When you take your dog to a trial, warm him up after you take him out of his crate. This could be done with an exercise he likes, such as playing ball or tug.
- Carry your dog over to the go-to-ground area. Let him watch other dogs go into the hole. Let him see that they are taken away from the rats. Be happy and encouraging during the entire process. Remember that you are communicating to him that this is fun, not torture.
- After your dog performs, walk him for maybe ten minutes or more before crating him again. Jog him around, play tug with him, help him burn off that adrenaline. Allow him to return to his normal state, to no longer be loaded, cocked, and ready to fire.
- When you do crate him, put a toy in the crate with him. This toy should be something he really likes. Kong, Rhino, or another toy that allows you to jam a cookie or peanut butter inside of it works well. Now the crate time is not so

unpleasant. Terminator can lick the peanut butter and work on wedging free that precious cookie!

There are many other games that we play with our terriers that can spark an adrenaline response and cause them to become dangerous. Not just racing, but agility and even regular play. Keep your eyes peeled for dilated pupils and a pounding heart. When your Terrier gets that "cocked and loaded look" he is ready to fire. However unacceptable to us; Terriers that bite under those circumstances are being a very normal dog. Use the guidelines above to find an aggression prevention strategy for your dog. There are many more reasons that a dog might be aggressive other than a surge of adrenaline or canine play targeted toward humans. An important consideration in terms of dog aggression; is having your Terrier checked medically for thyroid, or other disorders that might be causing him pain or discomfort. After all, if you did not feel well you would be grumpy too.

No matter what causes a Terrier to be aggressive, we as owners bear the responsibility to teach our dogs alternative behaviors. Any aggression problem is our responsibility to fix. Even if it's not our dog, we all bear the responsibility to stop unacceptable aggression. After all, we live in a crazy world where normal dog behavior is penalized with capital punishment. There is no second chance. Make a difference now!

Same-sex aggression and aggression towards other breeds of dogs is well documented with this breed. It is strongly recommended that no more than two Jack Russell's of opposite sex ever be permitted to stay together unattended. It is not wise to leave two Jack's of the same sex together.

- Most behavioral problems are due to a lack of companionship, discipline, activity and exercise.
- For a Jack Russell that is very aggressive with other dogs, a technique is to squirt the terrier in the face with water whenever he growls at other dogs. No scolding or other action is required in this instance - just a surprise squirt.
- A Jack Russell Terrier that bites can be a big problem. You must stop this behavior before it becomes dangerous.
- Don't allow your Jack Russell to win any games of aggression. The outcome could certainly send the wrong message to him.
- Exercise, exercise, exercise! A tired dog seldom wants to pick a fight.
- Never put your hands between two fighting terriers
- Jack Russell's require firm, consistent discipline. They are extremely intelligent; continue to test their limits throughout their life.
- Jack Russell's can become very possessive of their owner or a favorite member of the family. They will also be possessive over whatever they consider to be their personal property if allowed to do so. Aggressive behavior must be controlled from an early age.
- Jack Russell's can be very destructive if left unattended.

The typical dominant dog will growl if you try to move him aside, growl in bed at night if you move, refuse to get off the furniture when told, will not roll over on his/her back and will growl if you attempt it, will attempt to mount, a.k.a. hump, a human, food/toy/treat protection, barking as a form of demanding something from you, among many other things. Some dogs will do one of the above and not be a serious problem, but when you put several together there is a problem. If any of the situations above are happening in your home, you need to get a handle on it right away. Don't wait until it gets worse or until someone is bitten. The sooner you get a grip on the situation, the better.

The first things I suggest are keeping the dog off of the furniture at all times. No sleeping in bed, no getting on the couch, chairs, etc. This is allowing the dog to be your equal. Some dogs can handle sleeping in bed with you without letting it get to their head, but it is best not to tempt fate in the first place. Control the food. You decide when the dog eats. For a dog with serious issues, feed the dog by hand. Make the dog work for his meals. Don't just toss the food in a bowl and let him have at it. Have him "sit" or any other command, and then give him a few pieces of food. Do the same until the food is gone. If the dog refuses to obey the command, the food goes up and that's it for that meal. A dog that's hungry will learn to obey commands if they want to eat. Being in charge of the food shows that you are in control, and you are alpha in the house. The same goes for toys and treats. The dog has to earn them. Do not give an unlimited supply. Keep toys hidden and when the dog has behaved very well, let him have one toy.

As Dr. Nicholas Dodman states in his book, *Dogs Behaving Badly* there is "No free lunch." The dog has to earn everything from food to affection. Do not let your dog come to you and nudge you for attention. That puts them in control of the situation. Don't praise continuously. Praise right after he has obeyed a command. The dog needs to understand what you want from him. You can't just correct for bad behavior without teaching the dog what good behavior is.

Another thing to remember is always control play time. If you're playing fetch, you must initiate the game or it doesn't get played. You also determine when it ends. If the dog refuses to bring the ball back and wants to play chase, turn around and walk in the house and the game is over. Dominant dogs love to have control of every situation. Remember to avoid confrontation at this point. If you know that something sets off the dog, try to avoid it. You're trying to teach the dog what is "good" and acceptable behavior.

If a dog is truly aggressive, do not attempt to scruff or alpha roll the dog. An inexperienced person can get seriously injured attempting to do this. In the early stages of aggression, a dog that's just testing the waters to see what he can get away with. Put him in his place right away. Don't wait until you're getting bitten and are fearful of the dog. Dogs sense fear and if your dog knows he can push your buttons, he will do it happily. Body language is very important when dealing with dogs. This is a major way they communicate. Petting a dominant dog on the top of the head can set a dog off.

Also consult Dr. Dodman's book *The Dog Who Loved Too Much* for behavioral issues. There are other good books, but the best way to find them if to take action and search them out. Also, I strongly suggest finding a trainer to evaluate the dog and your situation at home. Coming to your home and seeing firsthand what is going on is always a plus. Make sure the trainer is experienced with terriers and aggression. The wrong trainer can make a situation worse. For minor problems I suggest getting into an obedience class ASAP. It helps create a bond and also teaches the dog that you are in charge.

Nipping and biting is how a puppy explores its world and learns its boundaries.

When you allow a puppy to nip or bite at you, or your clothes, without an appropriate correction or consequences, you are actually teaching this youngster that it is acceptable behavior. Not a good idea in the long run. Time outs work great for teaching the puppy that if they can't play nicely, they can't play at all. For puppies that bite there are two types of corrections that work well. It's not recommended discipline to be hitting a puppy or holding a puppy's mouth closed for biting. Instead put your hand over their muzzle and just push the lips into the teeth, if they exert pressure downward, they only end up biting themselves. This does two things; it gives them a correction, and simulates another dog putting its mouth over their muzzle. This mimics a common sign of dominance among canines, allowing you to reemphasize your dominance over them. You can also use a little pinch on the lip as a correction. With both corrections, give a verbal correction "No bite" and when they stop, praise them.

With patience and perseverance, you will eventually be able to give only a verbal correction and have them stop. With puppies, it's often a good idea to quickly distract them with an appropriate chew toy so they don't go right back to "finger attack" mode. If the corrections don't seem to work, then give time out, because they are either too wound up or too tired and need a nap. It might seem endless, but keep up the corrections needed to win this battle. Be persistent and they'll soon learn that nipping isn't such a fun game after all.

Separation Anxiety

There are three simple steps to help your dog overcome separation anxiety.
1. Before leaving, pay no attention to the dog for 20 - 30 minutes and leave a special toy or treat to distract the dog when you go out and remove the item upon your return.
2. When returning home, ignore your dog until he is quiet and relaxed and then interact on your own initiative. Do not reprimand your dog for destructive behavior such as urinating or defecating in the house.
3. While you are home, interact with your dog only at your initiative and when the dog is relaxed. Teach your dog to stay calm as you move away, gradually increasing the distance and time away. Put your coat on or play with your keys at times other than before you are going to depart.

Separation Anxiety is identifiable by one or more of the following: Excessive vocalization, excessive salivation, shaking, trembling, loss of interest in food if the owner is not present, urinating/defecating in the home, destruction, and in extreme cases self mutilation. Separation anxiety is a behavior that without behavior modification will only become worse. If these few steps do not help out, it is best to talk with your vet about other treatments, or contact a behavior specialist. In addition consider leaving the TV on or playing music while you are away; possibly placing a t-shirt or something with your scent on it near the crate so your terrier can smell it. It's possible that your scent will help calm him/her.

What separates a bored dog from one who suffers from separation anxiety? The term is used frequently by people who are looking for an explanation for destructive behavior when their dog is left alone. The distinction, however, is that separation anxiety is exactly that, Anxiety. A dog that causes destruction in your home is not necessarily an anxious dog, but could very well be a bored one. Many inexperienced pet owners will write off destructive behavior as separation anxiety until they have an encounter with the real thing. There is a huge difference between a bored dog chewing up a carpet and a dog with separation anxiety having a full blown panic attack. A bored dog will remain calm and sedate while lazily chewing on your belongings for hours. A dog with separation anxiety will rip your clothing to shreds in a fit, leaving pieces scattered to all four corners of the room and shaking whatever remains of his target furiously. A Jack Russell Terrier with separation anxiety is like the Tasmanian Devil from Bugs Bunny. These dogs will attack objects, not just casually chew. Owners with dogs that suffer from this condition often come home to a new layer of carpeting made up of pillow stuffing and shredded upholstery. The debris will look like a war zone.

Anxiety is also characterized by trembling, salivation, and even refusal of food. A dog with serious separation anxiety will most likely not even be able to eat when the owner is not present. Even if you put the dog in a crate and give them bowls of food and water, if they have separation anxiety you'll often come home to them running back and forth in the cage banging into and gnawing at the bars, with the water spilt and the food untouched.

Self destruction is another symptom. A dog can be so intensely stressed that he won't feel the pain he is inflicting on himself. Many owners who think that the dog will discover how to deal with their emotional issues by learning to be alone and getting used to it are poorly misguided. Owners who take this approach to training will often come home to find a dog that has banged around in the cage to the point of injury, some will even be able to work a small sharp edge around the bars, latch, or corners free and end up inflicting bloody wounds to them selves that will need immediate medical attention. These symptoms are a giant flashing billboard that the dog is more than just bored and will often leave owners distraught and beside themselves with worry.

Boredom can usually be cured with exercise, or leaving a dog in a crate with a nice toy to keep him busy. He may bark at you when you leave, but eventually he'll settle down. Anxiety isn't that simple. It is strongly recommended that anyone with an anxious dog seek professional help. The severity differs from dog to dog and not all require the same solution, but here are a few suggestions that will help with mild cases of separation anxiety.

- **Crate your dog safely.** It's much less overwhelming and stressful for a dog to be confined to his own, safe den. An empty house can seem enormous and even frightening for a dog suffering from anxiety. Crating is also a great way to keep the dog away from items he can destroy so that when you come home you won't be angry because you have a huge mess to clean up. Plan feeding schedules so the dog won't have to defecate in the crate while you're gone! Some anxious dogs just can't hold it!
- **Avoid emotional hellos and goodbyes.** Believe it or not, people can really worsen anxiety by putting their dog into emotional overload just before they leave and when they return home. Jack Russell's are so much more prone to being affected by this than the average low-key dog. Keep arrivals and departures emotionless.

- **Train your dog in basic obedience.** Basic obedience training is so helpful in showing a dog his spot in the "pack" or family. A well trained dog is less likely to be subjected to lots of highs and lows. One minute he's a good boy, and the next minute he's driving you nuts. Those highs and lows really worsen anxiety.
- **Seek professional advice.** Some vets will prescribe psychotropic drugs as well as behavior modification for dogs with separation anxiety.
- **Be Patient and Consistent** There is nothing more important in having a healthy relationship with your dog than consistency and patience. It will take you a long way in communicating with your dog and building a strong bond of trust. Very often, anxiety is increased by a family where there is a good cop/bad cop mentality; where one spouse is easy and the other is tough. See to it that your whole family follows the same consistent rules pertaining to your dog.

Submissive Urination

To begin with, submissive urination is not a house-training problem. A weak bladder causes it when the dog is excited or frightened. That is why it's seen most often in younger dogs. Submissive urination occurs in both male and female dogs, but is more common in the latter. Submissive urination occurs when a dog feels threatened, such as when it's being punished or verbally scolded. It may also occur when someone is reaching for it from a dominant posture, such as using direct eye contact and leaning forward over the dog. Excitement urination occurs most often during greetings and play and is not accompanied by submissive posturing. These two forms of urination are easily diagnosed depending on the context of which they occur. There are several things that the owner can do to help stop both of these behaviors.

1. No punishment or scolding should be used. It will only make the problem worse.
2. Keep greetings low-key when returning home.
3. Avoid approaching the dog in a dominant posture by:
   o Avoiding direct eye contact. Dogs assume that direct eye contact is a challenge. For a submissive dog, even a moment's eye contact can be intolerable.
   o bending down to the dog's level rather than leaning over to pet
   o Petting from under the chin rather than on top of the head. Dominant dogs often display their control by placing their neck or a paw over another dog's neck or shoulders. When a human pats a dog on the head, a submissive dog perceives it as a display of dominance.
4. Encourage and reward postures and behaviors that are exclusive of urination. In other words, give them something else to do rather than rolling over and urinating on the floor.
5. Ignore the dog until it is calm. This may prevent urination. If this does work, you can try adding some very calm words of greeting and gradually add physical affection over the next few minutes. After the physical affection, if your Jack Russell has still has not urinated, tell him/her "good boy/girl" and give them a treat.

Submissive and excitement urination may resolve on their own as the dog matures, if it's not made worse with punishment or inadvertent reinforcement. After trying out these suggestions a couple of times, if you are still having a problem with submissive/excitement urination I would suggest that you have your veterinarian check the animal to rule out any urinary tract infections.

Picky Eaters

If you are having problems getting your dog to eat and/or have a picky eater, here are some guidelines that may help. This method should be used for approximately two weeks. Once it becomes routine for the dog, he will eat when the food is put down. Please remember that eating habits are usually created by humans and dogs are not naturally picky eaters. Please don't add anything to the food, such as canned food or gravy, but adding water is acceptable.

First put the food down. If it's not completely gone in 15 minutes pick it up and wait until the next feeding. Feed twice a day so that if the dog didn't eat in the morning he has a chance to eat that evening. If the dog doesn't eat that evening, pick up the food and wait until the morning. If you feed once a day, it's hard to stick to that schedule if the dog doesn't eat on his first offer. If you're firmly set on feeding once a day for some reason, then be firm and consistent from the start; only offer food once per day. If they don't eat, offer the food again at the same time on the following day. Be sure that you actually have a reason for wanting to restrict feedings to once a day and not because you just "heard it somewhere".

You have to be patient and consistent with this. Do not worry about the dog starving. No healthy dog will allow itself to starve to death. It's not going to hurt the dog to miss a couple of meals, but it will show the dog that he/she has to eat when you put the food down for him/her. During this time do not give any extras, such as treats. Remember that you are trying to get this dog to eat when you want it and not when it wants to eat. If you follow this routine your dog will more than likely be eating normally within two weeks. It has worked in the past and will work for you if you are consistent in your feeding practices. Remember that consistency is the key to everything with a Jack Russell.

House Breaking

Housebreaking in theory is very simple. It's finding a means of preventing the puppy from doing his duties in the house, and giving him only an opportunity to do it outside. A dog is a strong creature of habit and because he learns by association, he will soon know there is no other place to relieve himself but the great outdoors. If you are experiencing issues with house breaking, below are some tips and questions to consider.

- Determine if it is physical or a mental problem. To check if physical problem, see your vet. This is especially important if your previously well-behaved dog has begun house soiling.
- Give your Jack Russell plenty of exercise. Exercise is not a luxury to a Jack Russell, it's a must.
- Examine the type and quality of the food you are feeding your terrier. Is it a good quality food? It may have too much soy or corn.

- Are you allowing free choice feeding? Is there always food out? This is usually not a good practice. Feed puppies three times a day and adults twice a day. After 10 to 15 minutes, withdraw the food.
- Do not give the puppy any food after 6 pm. It takes a dog about 6 hours to digest his food and experience elimination as a result of that meal. Any food after 6 pm may give him an unexpected urge after he is put to bed.
- Always get your dog outside after feeding!
- Are you using a crate to help to train the puppy? Take advantage of a very natural instinct of the dog, his desire to keep his sleeping quarters clean and not to mess where he sleeps.
- Always have fresh clean water available during the day. If your dog is inclined to night soil or urinate in the house, use a crate for the night. Do not over crate or use the crate for punishment. Make it comfortable for the dog.
- Get your dog outside to relieve itself on a regular basis. Don't forget how important it is to praise a Jack Russell. They are very praise oriented.
- Are you giving the dog the complete run of the house? It might be better to restrict the area of the house free to the dog.
- It helps to train a Jack Russell to soil and urinate in the same small area. Have a specific area that the dog is taken to relieve itself. They will catch on more quickly.
- First thing in the morning, pick the puppy up and take him outside to relieve himself.
- In spite of a rigid routine, your pup may have an occasional accident during his periods of freedom. Here is where correction is necessary. If you catch him in the act, with a loud "NO" put him outside at once. Remember, a dog learns by association and in connection with any act of wrong doing, he must receive some form of discomfort in order to learn that he has done wrong. However, you must catch him in the act - it does absolutely no good to punish him for a mistake he has made an hour or even five minutes earlier.

Prevent Your Puppy's Destructive Chewing

It's perfectly natural for puppies to want to explore their surroundings. Two primary ways of getting to know the world around them are through their noses and mouths, which is why many puppies can be seen smelling or chewing on just about everything they encounter.

Preventing Destructive Chewing Using a Constructive Multi-Pronged Approach

Many new dog owners will attempt to discipline their puppy for wrong doing after the fact. This usually consists of an owner coming home to find a chewed up mess that occurred during their absence. In many cases the chewing and the discipline continues with no improvement. Many desperate owners will go out and spend a bundle of money on a massive amount of chew toys in order to keep the dog distracted from valuable belongings. This does work, but not for long. The dog will be in love with their new toys for 2 or 3 days, but after awhile they will return to chewing on the sofa that they are familiar with. Many professional obedience trainers will come into the home and notice that it looks like a toy store for dogs. Clearly, neither after-the-fact discipline nor truckloads worth of puppy toys are the answer. Instead follow this multi-prong approach to correcting a puppy's chewing problem:

1. **Puppy-proof your home**. Instead of constantly reprimanding a young puppy for getting into things, puppy-proof any areas of the house to which your puppy will be given access, in much the same way one would child-proof an area for a baby:
   o Temporarily take up any throw rugs.
   o Place all plants, poisonous substances, household cleaners, trash receptacles, paper products, shoes, and any small chewable objects out of reach.
   o Remove, cover, or tape down all accessible electrical wires.
   o Remove or secure heavy objects which could fall or be pulled down and cause injury to the puppy.

2. **Limit the number of toys**. While all puppies should have toys to play with, there is a problem with providing your puppy with too many toys. It becomes difficult for the puppy to differentiate what's his from what's yours. Do not provide a destructive puppy with more than a few toys at a time. This rule doesn't apply to dogs who are not destructive chewers.

3. **Safely confine your puppy**. Use a suitably sized crate or wire-reinforced puppy gate whenever you're unable to safely supervise him. When introduced properly and used correctly, crate training is a safe, preventive, effective, and a humane housetraining tool. The crate provides the puppy with a secure, protective den, while offering his owner peace of mind. Please note: Introduce your puppy to his new crate using positive association. Feed him in his crate, and never use his crate as a punishment.

4. **Offer him lots of outdoor exercise**. Puppies that are destructive indoors need between one and two hours of daily active outdoor exercise, provided they are fully immunized. Teaching your puppy to retrieve a ball, toy, or Frisbee will help cure his chronic chewing problem. If your puppy doesn't have all of his shots yet, it's probably not safe to allow him to play with other dogs, other than those who are already part of your household, or to give him any access to outdoor areas where neighborhood dogs go. Final puppy shots are usually administered by a veterinarian when a puppy is around 16 weeks of age.

5. **Offer your (fully vaccinated) puppy playtime with a puppy playmate**. Lots of active play each day keeps a hyperactive puppy from being a terror at home.

6. **Obedience train your puppy.** Just 5 to 15 minutes of training a day can make a big difference. For young, immature and hyperactive puppies that have difficulty concentrating during lengthy obedience lessons, even a few 30-second obedience training "mini-sessions" offered on a daily basis will prove very helpful. Remember to remain upbeat throughout, and always end your sessions on a positive note. There are several ways you can learn how to train your dog, including:
   o training books and videos
   o group obedience classes
   o private in-home training
   o training seminars

7. **Enroll your (vaccinated) puppy in an agility training class.** Agility training helps build coordination and confidence, offers your puppy substantial exercise, and is great fun.
8. **Apply Bitter Apple spray or salve to accessible woodwork and furniture legs.** The bitter taste is usually an effective deterrent for most puppies.
9. **Avoid the futile after-the-fact discipline syndrome.** In order to successfully correct your puppy's misbehavior, you must either catch your puppy in the act, or, better yet, work on preventing his misbehavior to begin with.
10. **Consider enlisting the help of a reputable dog trainer or canine behavioral consultant.** If despite these steps your puppy still acts like a canine demolition crew.

Choose Suitable Chew Toys

Rather than attempting to stifle your puppy's chewing tendencies, his desire to chew should be constructively channeled and directed towards acceptable items such as his chew toys. Avoid giving your puppy discarded socks, shoes, sneakers or other articles of clothing. While some puppies may learn to differentiate between those things which are his and those which are yours, most puppies cannot. When it comes to choosing which toys to give your puppy, these are the primary qualities to look for:

- **Safety**. Only allow him those toys and balls which cannot be chewed apart or accidentally swallowed. Also, beware of bells, buttons and squeakers, which may be hazardous if chewed off of a toy and swallowed.
- **Durability.** Good chew toys should last a long time.
- **Fun**. If it's not fun, your puppy won't want to play with it.
- **Ease of cleaning**. After all, who wants to spend all of their time cleaning chew toys?

Some professionally recommended toys:

- The Tuffy or Kong. These are not only great chew toys, but are also great retrieve toys as well. They have plenty of "give" for puppies who are teething, and are also virtually indestructible for most dogs. Two of the best puppy toys on the market.
- Cresite, Beefy Baseball, or other durable rubber balls. Both the solid and hollow thick rubber balls can be rolled across floor for puppy to chase and chew.
- Tennis balls are perfect for teaching medium to large sized puppies to retrieve.
- Starballs. These odd-shaped, erratic-bouncing balls are ideal for the consummate retriever who likes a bit of a challenge.
- Mutt Pucks, which are both hardy enough to last with most puppies, yet are not too hard as to discourage chewing. Some dogs can chew their toys apart in a surprisingly short period of time. Should this happen with your puppy, remove any pieces which can be swallowed immediately.
- Buster Cubes and Activity Balls. Fill these toys with kibble or your puppy's favorite treats and watch the fun begin.
- For special occasions, make "Puppy Cannoli's": hollowed, sterilized beef marrow bones, which can be filled with a thick kibble-based mixture, then frozen.

To make the mixture, place I cup dry dog food kibble, 1 small cube of freeze-dried liver, crushed into powder, 1 teaspoon powdered or fresh pressed garlic, and 1 cup warm water. Mix well and let sit for 1 hour. Stuff the mixture into beef marrow bone. Cover edges with approx.1 tablespoon cream cheese or soft Velveeta cheese (optional). Freeze overnight. Frozen "Puppy Cannoli's" should be considered an extra special treat, and offered only on an occasional basis. Make sure the beef marrow bone is big enough that it can't be swallowed, and that bone fragments are not eaten. Owner supervision is advised.

Crating Your Terrier

Crate training is an excellent training tool. Any wild canine will secure a small, snugly fitting space to call its own. This space represents security to the dog. In its den, it cannot be attacked or bothered, so it's able to relax fully. This instinctive desire for a secure den is the basis of the psychology behind using a crate as a training aid.

Guidelines for Crating Puppies and Older Dogs

- 9-10 Weeks - Approx. 30-60 minutes
- 11-14 Weeks - Approx. 1-3 hours
- 15-16 Weeks - Approx. 3-4 hours
- 17+ Weeks - Approx. 4+ (6 hours maximum)

Important Points:

- To accustom your dog to its new crate, prop open the door and allow the dog to explore the confines of the crate.
- The dog can be confined for up to **four** hours at a time.
- **No dog should be left in its crate for the entire day.**
- Both you and your dog should think of the crate as a safe haven, not as a prison.
- Many dogs receive their meals in their crates.
- A healthy dog will not soil its den.
- If you purchase a crate for a puppy based on the size of the mature dog, you may need to block off one end to keep the puppy from sleeping in one corner and using the other for elimination.
- Any time you cannot keep a close watch on the puppy, kindly place it in its crate.
- The crate is a safety seat for a traveling dog.
- A crate-trained dog is relaxed and less likely to need sedation for traveling.
- No untrained dog should be given the run of the house while its owner is away.
- Use a crate to protect the untrained dog from itself.

In dozens of different ways, the addition of a crate means better care for your dog. It reinforces consistency in training. It helps the dog feel more secure. It makes having strangers in the house less hectic. It makes travel safer and more comfortable. It makes bringing up a puppy as easy as it can be. Once you have experienced the benefits of crate-training your dog, you will question how you ever lived without that marvelous crate.

The Negative Effects of Chasing Flashlights for Exercise

The Jack Russell Terrier is an earth working breed. This means that their very nature is centered on hunting. What makes this terrier so alert and bright is the fact that they're ready for anything to come their way; after all, it takes a bold, highly intelligent dog to find his way through the earth to either bolt or keep a fox at bay. A fox is a treacherous enemy for any dog not equipped for the confrontation both mentally and physically.

When a Jack Russell Terrier does his/her job in the earth, he/she needs the senses of sight, scent and sound, not one or the other, but all of the above. Imagine taking all those keen senses and limiting them to sight only. Basically, that's what allowing a dog to hunt a beam of light is doing. The effect this will have on a terrier will be one of confusion. Very rarely can a terrier fully understand that the beam of light comes from a flashlight or laser light alone, and more often than not, they begin to think they see the light when their owner isn't even holding the mechanism that creates it. When this happens, the owner has succeeded in causing Obsessive Compulsive Disorder (OCD) in their dog. Can you just imagine how confusing it is to a dog that something that attracts your sense of sight is so unexpected that you can't smell it, taste it, hear it, or otherwise sense it? It's just this phenomenon you see, but cannot sense in any other way. The dog will begin chasing things around the house like the flash of car headlights coming through a window, or even the glint of light off a watch. Some rescue dogs cannot ride in a car at night because the shadows created by oncoming car headlights send them into a total tizzy. Sadly, dogs are given up because their own owners have created OCD in the animal that they can't deal with any longer. This occurs more often than you'd think. Owners are not being cruel; they simply have no idea what they're creating with this game.

There's a great chapter on this in Nicolas Dodman's book *The Dog Who Loved Too Much*. It's titled "Chasing Rabbits," and tells of a Bassett Hound who was given up because of the OCD caused by chasing a flashlight beam. Caroline Coile also addresses the topic in her latest book, *Jack Russell Terriers Complete Owners Manual*. By all means, if you need to exercise your dog, try to find a way to do it without using a flashlight or laser beam.

Eating Grass

Grass eating can be due to several reasons. Some dogs will ingest grass to induce vomiting. If you notice your dog is continually eating grass to induce vomiting, we recommend that you take a trip to your Vet. Some dogs enjoy "grazing". There are several dogs who just like the taste of grass. It's not uncommon for a dog to grab a few blades of grass once in a while. If your lawn is chemically treated, try to keep the dog from eating grass. Also, if you go to a dog park or walks anywhere else, try to avoid grass eating for this reason. Some dogs like to run the blades through their mouth to "taste" it and don't actually eat the grass. If you have a dog that really enjoys eating grass you might want to add pureed veggies to their food or herbs. Please discuss any herbs with your veterinarian before feeding them to be sure they are safe.

Stool Eating

There can be several causes of stool eating (also known as Copropagia) in dogs. Terriers fed diets they can't properly digest will eat their stool because they consider it semi-digested food rather than waste. Dogs will also eat the stool of other animals whose waste displays similarly appealing characteristics. A change in diet will possibly solve this problem. Owners can become obsessed with a dog's stool, often due to a medical problem or when the owner takes a heavy handed, highly emotional approach to housebreaking. Your terrier may eat the stool to avoid dealing with your response to it. It's best to put your emotions on hold and seek to identify and eliminate the real cause of the behavior rather than merely eliminate the behavior itself. One way to cure the problem is to add a teaspoon of Crushed Pineapple to your dog food, the natural enzymes in the pineapple causes the stools to be less appealing and this will help if not stop the problem. This will take two or three weeks to see any results, so don't expect this to stop over night.

Recommended Reading

There are several books that are recommended to new owners of Jack Russell's. To make it easier on everyone, here is a list of some of the most highly suggested Jack Russell books. Happy reading!

- How to Housebreak Your Dog in Seven Days – Shirlee Kalstone
- The Evans Guide for Housetraining Your Dog – Job Michael Evans
- Childproofing Your Dog – Brian Kilcommons
- Dogs & Kids: Parenting Tips – Bardi McLennan
- Dr. Pitcairn's Complete Guide to Natural Health for Dogs and Cats – Dr. Richard H. Pitcairn
- People, Pooches and Problems – Job Michael Evans
- The Art of Raising a Puppy – The Monks of New Skete
- How to be Your Dog's Best Friend – New Skete Monks
- The Power of Positive Dog Training – Pat Miller
- Book of the Bitch – J.M. Evans
- Canine Reproduction – Phyllis A. Holst
- Successful Obedience Handling – Barbara S. Handler

Cats and Jack Russell's

Jack Russell's are commonly known to harass, injure or kill other small pets, such as cats, birds, rabbits, mice, rats, gerbils, etc. simply due to their strong natural hunting instincts. These instincts have been bred into the Jack Russell for hundreds of years contributing to what makes them such excellent working dogs in the field. Raising a Jack Russell puppy with a cat does not guarantee the cat's life-long safety. Don't be lulled into a false sense of security, there is often a "honeymoon" period of sometimes many years before mishaps occur. Please refer to the true-life testimonials below. If you do decide to co-exist with both a Jack Russell and a cat in the same household there are steps you should take to keep them both safe.

1. Discourage rough play.
2. Provide more than a few 'high areas' where the cat can jump up to for safety.

3. Never, ever leave them alone, unsupervised, indoors or out. This means separating them via kennels or closed doors every single time you leave the house without fail!

True Life Testimonials

"We had a beloved cat that lived peacefully with our three terriers for nine years. The Jacks and cat would occasionally play with each other, and whenever we thought the play was getting a bit too boisterous we'd break it up. We never left them alone together, kenneling two of the dogs and shutting the cat away in a room whenever we left the house. Then came that fateful day. We were in a rush to get out of the house and both of us thought the other had secured the cat in his 'room'. We arrived home five hours later and the one lone terrier (a trusted house pet) greeted us warmly at the door, acting as if nothing was wrong. What we found was our fat black kitty, dead on the dining room floor, with a broken neck...and signs of a great chase throughout the house. What made this ten times worse is that the cat was our daughter's pet. Could we blame ourselves for being careless? Absolutely. Could we blame the terrier for killing the cat? Absolutely not. I guess my point is that unless you are 100% vigilant, 100% of the time, this could easily happen to you".

Judy

"I have a sweet, loving, 16 month old spayed JRT. I also have two adult male cats. For the past 13 months my JRT has lived peacefully with my cats. They all were friends and got along great. When I read posts on this board about JRT's being unpredictable with cats, I laughed and said "Not MY JR! She loves her cat friends!" I also thought everyone who is a Forum assistant was crazy when they told people that JRT's and cats do not work. I came home today to find one of my male cats in bad shape. He has two large cuts on his head and stomach from where my JRT became aggressive with him. He had to have over 50 stitches and it cost me over $200 in vet bills. My JRT and cat never had any previous problems. They were best friends, and all slept with me every night. PLEASE LISTEN TO ME! JRT's are hunting animals! If you do not want to go through what I have been through today, PLEASE KEEP YOUR JRT AWAY FROM YOUR CATS! My poor cat is very sore and luckily he survived. My entire living room (new light green carpet) is covered in his blood, and I think if I hadn't gotten home when I did, I would have found him dead. I know it was my JRT because she had blood over her mouth and paws. My other cat was hiding, terrified, behind the couch, and he didn't come out for over 2 hours.
You don't want to go through what I have gone through. I have left my JRT and cats alone for 13 months, and had NO PREVIOUS PROBLEMS. It is not worth it."

Anonymous

Jack Russell's and Children

Jack Russell Terriers are not good with small children, and are not recommended for families with children under the age of eight. Young children are not mature enough to differentiate between a stuffed toy and a living, breathing animal. They are not capable of controlling their impulses, and can be overly rough with a dog who will feel the need to protect himself, usually by biting the child. Small children also move quickly, squeak, squeal, and to a dog, smell funny. All of these things can be overwhelming and frightening to an energetic terrier who is easily excited.

Please read the information at the beginning of this chapter on aggression as well as other chapters of this book in order to learn how to deal with displays of aggression appropriately. Children under the age of eight should never be left alone with a dog. Don't allow the children to handle or pet the dog around the face, muzzle, or head. No grabbing of the tail or legs and feet either. Teach your children the proper way to handle and pet a dog. Make sure that your dog has a safe place to go where the children are not permitted. It's a good idea to get your children more involved in the care and training of the dog. This will give them a better understanding and respect for the dog.

Never punish the dog for biting a child. First, separate the child and dog in different areas so you can attend to the child without distractions. Do not send another child to move the dog to another room as they too may get bit. Children have a tendency to want to get even with the dog. Make sure that they know this will only confuse the dog, and make him bite again. Talk with the child who was bitten, and find the cause of the sudden aggression. Discuss with the child what they could've done differently.

Having a new baby in the home can greatly confuse a dog. If you are going to change you or your dog's routines, now is the time to do it, not after a baby arrives. Try to make this as gradual as possible. If your dog is not obedience trained, don't waste any time getting him enrolled. Do it now! This will also be good exercise for you while you are pregnant. Get your dog used to baby smells by using baby lotion and powder on your hands and body. Get a tape of babies crying from the Hospital where you will be delivering and play it at home. A few weeks before delivering start by playing the tape softly at intervals during the day and night. Increase the volume slightly every day. Reward him for behaving. Purchase a realistic baby doll to cuddle and attend to after you have played the tape for a week. Use the baby lotion and powder on the doll. Make sure to give the dog attention while you are playing with the doll, praise him for being good. Do not let him do more than sniff the doll. This is a good time to use what you have learned earlier in obedience class. When you are done attending to the doll, place it in the crib and ignore the dog. Only give him attention while you are giving the doll attention. This will help him make a positive association with the doll and soon the baby. When the baby comes you should remember this above all: if the baby cries, give attention to the dog first, but only if he is behaving. Same thing for the many guests that will be visiting you, the dog gets attention first. Here are a few suggested books to help with introducing your children to the dog.

- Your New Baby and Bowser, by Stephen Rafe
- Dogs and Kids: Parenting Tips, by Bardi McLennan
- Childproofing Your Dog; A Complete Guide to Preparing Your Dog for the Children In Your Life, by Brian Kilcommons

Jack Russell's and Other Breeds

There have been many questions as of late about Jack Russell and other breeds of dogs. This question cannot always be answered. Most Jack enthusiasts have only had experience with Jack Russell Terriers and recommending another breed is something they cannot do. Please make this your own decision to add another breed to your family. Be aware that Jack Russell's will not get along with all breeds. Good common sense will help you make the right decision. We recommend that you research both breeds that you are considering. Information about Jack Russell Terriers can be found throughout this book. Talk to your Breeders and follow their advice. You may want to get this advice in writing. In case it doesn't work out, you may return the Jack Russell or the other breed, to the breeder, whether it is 6 months or 6 years old. As much as we would like to help you in this matter - this must be your decision.

2nd Jack Russell

Same-sex aggression and aggression towards other breeds of dogs will be mentioned frequently in this book. It is the norm for Jack Russell's. If you do get a second dog, it would be a good thing to introduce them on neutral grounds. If the second dog is just a puppy, avoid the parks and the germs; try a neighbor's backyard, where you know the dogs are well vaccinated. It's important to discourage any show of dominance or aggression from the start. Give positive reinforcement for nice behavior on both sides. Be ready with praise or a treat.

If you are willing to manage two females, separately, if need be, then you can consider getting a second female. However, if you are not willing to take the steps to keep both of them safe, then it is best to pass on the idea for now. It may be fine now, but there could be considerable problems when they are older. Many owners have multiple females, but keep those that don't get along separated and never unsupervised. Some females will continue to fight for dominance with each other even after being spayed.

Chapter 4

Appearance and Standard of a Jack Russell

In most breeds, dog shows will judge them on appearance and their standard will directly relate to how the dog appears visually. This is not the case with the Jack Russell. Because it's a working Terrier, the Jack Russell is judged on its body dimensions and its ability to perform complex work tasks, not on their specific appearance. A key element in the evaluation of Jack Russell's is chest size. A strong barrel shaped chest that's still small enough to crawl into the den of any fox and work game from burrows is of the utmost importance.

The most common adversary of the Jack Russell is the Red Fox, which Reverend John Russell specifically created the modern day Jack Russell to hunt. The fox will make a home in any den hole available, whether it's their own burrow, a groundhog hold, a rabbit hole, even a vacant badger's den. They've also been known to live inside drain pipes and building crawl spaces. In any event, a proper Jack Russell must be small enough to chase a fox and fit into its home, no matter how small. Generally it is preferred for a Jack Russell to have a chest size that is no larger than that of the average fox. Around the world the average known red fox chest ranges from 12-14 inches, and a proper Jack Russell's chest should match that range accordingly. The weight of the average fox is 14 lbs., it's desirable to be able to match the weight of the fox as well, but a working Terrier will often exceed that number slightly because of the dense muscle that the breed is known for.

Barry Jones, the founding Chairman of the National Working Terriers Federation was once asked to contribute opinions for Kennel Club Members who wanted to bring the Jack Russell's (as Parson Russell's) into dog showing events. Although most working terrier breeders and organizations are against this, he did offer some guidelines as was quoted as saying:

> *"The chest is, without doubt, the determining factor as to whether a terrier may follow its intended quarry underground. Too large and he/she is of little use for underground work, for no matter how determined the terrier may be, this physical setback will not be overcome in the nearly-tight situations it will encounter in working foxes. It may be thought the fox is a large animal - to the casual observer it would appear so. However, the bone structure of the fox is finer than that of a terrier, plus it has a loose-fitting, profuse pelt which lends itself to flexibility. I have not encountered a fox which could not be spanned at 14 inches circumference - this within a weight range of 10 lbs to 24 lbs, on average 300 foxes spanned a year. You may not wish to work your terrier. However, there is a Standard to be attained, and spannability is a must in the Parson Russell Terrier."*

Modern day Jack Russell's should exhibit a coat that is more than 51% white and have black, tan, or tricolor patterns on their face and base of tail or lower back. The skin and first layer of undercoat fur should exhibit a pattern of black or brown freckles that do not show through to the surface of the fur. The rest of the skin that is not freckle should appear pink. The Jack Russell Terrier should have small "V" shaped ears. The ear should bend in the middle and flop forward toward the front of the head. The teeth of the Jack Russell should feature predominant upper and lower fangs, and all other teeth should be relatively sharp and pointed. The top teeth should cross over the bottom teeth like a pair of scissors. Jack Russell Terriers can feature one of several coats of fur.

The fur types are:
- Smooth – A short, thin, smooth layer of fur, about 1 to 1.5 cm long.
- Rough – a rougher, denser double coat of shaggy hair. Rough coats can be up to 10 cm long.
- Broken – a combination of the two. The coat can seem smoother and rougher in spots or can be consistently rough and shaggy like a rough coat, but usually much shorter. Fur is usually longer than 1.5 cm, but not more than 2.5-3 cm.

No matter what type of coat the fur should appear thick and dense, not linty of feathery. The Jack Russell's tail should be straight and point up toward the sky. The tail should be docked at five inches; this is because of the historic tradition of fox hunting. In the old hunting days, when a dog would get stuck in a hole while fox hunting, before the hunter would dig the dog out, the first option was to grab the dogs tail and pull. The tail should be strong and sturdy and not be painful to the dog if pulled by it gently and with proper training. Cutting the dog's tail too long is sometimes forgiven, but cutting it too short is an error and creates a less useful dog that may present issues with balance.

Many Jack Russell's have crooked or "benched" front legs that bend inward. This is considered to be a breeding defect which is a strike against the dog. Benched legs are a sign of Achondroplasia, a misalignment of bones and joints. Many dogs will not exhibit any problem from this, but an equal number will get progressively worse; joints will weaken and the dog will eventually become crippled.

A healthy Jack's forelegs should be straight, strong and with all joints in correct alignment. Elbows should hand perpendicular in relation to the body and swing free of the sides. The hindquarters should be strong and muscular with strong, pronounced angulations and bend of the muscle. The legs should be strong and able to give the Jack plenty of push while running. Looking from behind the sides of the body and legs should be straight. A Jack Russell should be generally square in appearance. His body should appear to have good proportion in relation to the length and height.

A good Working Terrier is a type, or strain, of terrier; not a "*pure bred*" in the sense that they have a broader gene pool than most breeds, a broad standard, and do not breed according to a specific look or characteristic. This is a result of having been bred strictly for hunting since their beginning in the early 1800's, and their preservation as a working breed since. The broad standard, varied genetic background based on years of restricted inbreeding and wide outcrossing, as well as great variety of size and type, are the major characteristics that make the Jack Russell (a.k.a. Parson Jack Russell Terrier) such a unique, versatile working terrier.

The core standard for a Jack Russell is as a fox hunting dog. This is where it derives its unique coloring, conformation, character, and intelligence from. The body is compact, balanced, has clean shoulders, straight legs, and most importantly, a small chest. The Jack Russell must also be totally flexible, allowing him to maneuver underground. This conformation allows the terrier to follow his quarry down narrow holes. The fox is a good model for the Jack Russell; where the fox can go, so must the terrier. Although originally bred for fox hunting, the Jack Russell has become a valuable tool in hunting groundhogs, raccoons, weasels, and even coyotes.

The best dogs do not score points for having a pretty face. There has been a great increase in the conformation showing of Jack Russell in recent years. Conformation exhibiting has been very effective in promoting correct conformation according to the breed standard, thereby improving the quality of the breeding stock. However, while showing is beneficial to the breed, JRTC trial events are designed to keep the working aspects of the terrier in the forefront. The highest awards presented to a terrier are its working awards; the Natural Hunting Certificate and the Bronze Medallion for Special Merit in the Field. National Trial Conformation Champion is selected from the JRTCA Working Terrier Division of the National Trial; all entries have proven their working ability to having earned at least one Natural Hunting Certificate in the field. Most sanctioned Jack Russell club judges are required to have experience working their terriers in the field, getting an in-depth, first-hand knowledge of terrier work, so they understand the importance of the physical characteristics necessary for a terrier to be useful for the work he was bred to do.

Why many Terrier Clubs do not approve of Kennel Club Recognition for Jacks

The Jack Russell Terrier Clubs of America (JRTCA), Canada (JRTCC) and Great Britain (JRTCB), as well as a large number of other Jack Russell Clubs, strongly oppose recognition of the Jack Russell by any Kennel Club/National All-Breed Registry. Most Jack Russell enthusiasts and Working Terrier people seem to be in complete agreement on this issue. Why are they against Kennel Club recognition?

These groups and Jack Russell caretakers feel that that Jacks' value is not in appearance and should not be graded in any kind of beauty pageant. They feel that doing so will weaken or compromise the working ability, intelligence, physical structure and problem solving skills needed to do the work that they are used for. These groups feel that the Jack's greatest value and importance is its ability to do work and take part in physical trials. They fear that if breeders begin to breed them to meet a certain look in order to meet show dog requirements that it will weaken or spoil the breeding stock, in turn endangering the usefulness, and endearing characteristics of the breed.

The Jack Russell has been bred for over 100 years as a working Terrier; it is an invaluable fox hunting tool to the huntsman of England for generations upon generations. Jack Russell enthusiasts know that Reverend Russell himself did not create the breed as we know it today to meet any kind of beauty standard, but to perform the specific tasks of hunting; a tradition many groups intend to uphold and protect. As one book so aptly described John Russell's Terriers, they were Fox Terriers bred to hunt fox.

When the Fox Terrier became recognized by the Kennel Club in the late 1800's, many unfamiliar with the dogs quickly tried to turn it into a new show breed darling. Several lines progressed (or some would say regressed) into a fancy show breed....and rapidly became one of the most popular breeds on the Kennel Club list. This dog show lines also quickly lost all usefulness as a Working Terrier. Breeding for form rather than function made rapid conformational changes in the breed; the shoulders straightened, the jaw became long and narrow, and the chest deepened to the point of preventing most descendants from ever entering an earth, assuming the owner would want them to. In turn their instincts began to weaken after years of breeding only for show.

True lovers of the Fox Terrier and stringent hunters continued to uphold the standard and bred John Russell's strain of Fox Terriers as John Russell had intended, for hunting fox. These lines are sound, with good small chests, angulations, and well placed shoulders, that enable them to move correctly and with agility above and below ground. They are able to go anywhere a fox can go. They are extremely intelligent, loyal, and of a perfect temperament for rousing fox from hidey holes. To these purists a real Jack Russell is simply an extension of the early, unspoiled strain of Fox Terriers; kept sound through years of breeding strictly for temperament, intelligence, and working ability.

As of February 1st, 1996, the JRTCC began a new Breed Registry. A terrier is not eligible for registration with the JRTCC in the Breed Register until it reaches one year of age, has reached full adult height, all adult teeth have come in and other aspects considered for full maturity. The individual applying for "Registration" must adhere to the breed standard. The "Register" will not accept Terriers with genetic or breeding defects. Above all things, the JRTCA and JRTCC prize the quality of their breed registers. Jack Russell enthusiasts disapprove of the Kennel Club register, because it does not reject dogs on the basis of genetic defect. Jack enthusiasts feel that the Kennel Club implicitly condones the breeding or defective gene pools by allowing dogs with genetic defects into their register. By rejecting dogs with inherited defects, Jack Russell clubs feel that they protect the Jack Russell and eliminate serious faults in the breed. Kennel Club registers do accept dogs which are product of Brother/Sister, mother/son or father/daughter mating. This sort of inbreeding has contributed to the physical and mental downfall of many breeds, making them unsuitable for work or companionship. The Register of North American Jack Russell clubs do permit very limited, often distant "inbreeding"; a restrictive practice to avoid problems.

Since its acceptance by the Kennel Club, the Fox Terrier has undergone many conformational changes as a result of the whims of the show ring; resulting in today's Modern Fox Terrier. John Russell maintained his strain of fox terriers bred strictly for working, and the terrier we know of today as the Jack Russell is much the same as the pre-1900 fox terrier. It's interesting to note that although John Russell was one of the original founders of England's Kennel Club in 1873, judged Fox Terriers in Kennel Club sanctioned shows, and remained a Kennel Club member for the rest of his life; he never showed his own dogs. The Jack Russell has survived the changes that have occurred in the modern-day Fox Terrier because it has been preserved by working terrier enthusiasts in England for more than 100 years; it has survived on its merit as a working terrier. It is the foremost goal of the JRTCA that the Jack Russell continued in that tradition. In 2001 the modern Fox Terrier line, that exhibited alterations due to show breeding, had its name changed to the Parson Russell Terrier.

If one takes a little time to research breeds that are recognized, it would not take long to compile long lists of genetic physical faults in many breeds. The list of working breeds that no longer work or no longer even resemble their working ancestors in physical or mental characteristics continues to grow annually. Jack Russell enthusiasts feel that the strength of the Jack Russell line needs to be protected and that by maintaining a close regulation on all breeding that it accepts into it circles, it will prevent the loss of one of the finest hunting dogs in history.

Jack Russell Terrier Basic Reference Information:

Breed:	Terrier
Size:	10 - 15 inches
Weight:	9 - 18 pounds
Coat Color:	White with black, tan, or black & tan markings
Coat Type:	Smooth, wire or broken coat, weather resistant
Origination:	England
Nicknames:	Puddin', Puds, Shorties
Lifespan:	13 - 18 years

The Jack Russell Terrier Standard
- **CHARACTER**: The Terrier must present a lively, active and alert appearance. It should impress with its fearless and happy disposition. It should be remembered

that the Jack Russell is a Working Terrier and should retain these instincts. Nervousness, cowardice or over-aggressiveness should be discouraged, and the terrier should always appear confident.

- **GENERAL APPEARANCE**: A sturdy, tough terrier, very much on its toes all the time, measuring 10" to 15" at the withers. The body length must be in proportion to the height, and should present a compact, balanced image, always being in solid, hard condition.
- **HEAD**: well balanced and in proportion to the body. The skull should be flat, of moderate width at the ears, narrowing to the eyes with a defined stop but not over pronounced. The length of the muzzle from the nose to the stop should be slightly shorter than the distance from the stop to the occiput. The nose should be black. The jaw should be powerful and well boned with strongly muscled cheeks.
- **EYES**: almond shaped dark in color, lively and intelligent.
- **EARS**: Small "V" shaped drop ears carried forward close to the head and of moderate thickness.
- **MOUTH**: Strong teeth with the top slightly overlapping (i.e."Scissors Bite", where upper incisors strike just along the front face of the lower ones). A level bite is acceptable, but overshot and undershot jaws are unregisterable. This is because the dog's teeth are meant for tearing and the dog's work would require increased effort.
- **NECK**: Clean and muscular, of good length, gradually widening at the shoulders.
- **FOREQUARTERS**: The shoulders should be sloping and well laid back, fine at points and clearly cut at the withers. Forelegs should be strong and straight boned with joints hanging perpendicular to the body and working free of the sides.
- **BODY**: The chest should be shallow, narrow and the front legs set not too widely apart, giving an athletic, rather than heavy chested appearance. As a guide only, the chest should be easily spanned behind the shoulders, by average sized hands, when the terrier is in a fit, working condition. The back should be strong, straight and, in comparison to the height of the terrier, give a balanced image. The loin should be slightly arched.
- **HINDQUARTERS**: Should be strong and muscular, well put together with good angulations and bend of stifle, giving plenty of drive and propulsion. Looking from behind, the hocks must be straight.
- **FEET**: Round, hard padded, of cat-like appearance, neither turning in or out.
- **TAIL**: Should be set rather high, carried gaily and in proportion to body length, usually about four inches long, providing a good hand-hold.
- **COAT**: Smooth, without being so sparse as not to provide a certain amount of protection from the elements and undergrowth. Rough or broken, without being woolly.
- **COLOUR**: White should predominate (i.e., dog must be more than 51% white with tan, black or brown markings). Brindle and grey markings are unacceptable.
- **GAIT**: Movement should be free, lively, well-coordinated with straight action in front and behind.

NOTE: For showing purposes, terriers are classified into two groups: 10" to 12 1/2" and 12 1/2" to 15". Old scars and injuries should not be allowed to prejudice a terrier's chance in the show ring, unless they interfere with its movement or with its utility for work or stud. Male dogs should have two apparently normal testicles fully descended into the scrotum.

Some Variations you may see in a Jack Russell and other tips

Prick Ears

The condition called "prick ears" consists of a pup's ears standing up instead of folding forward. This is usually a permanent condition. The JRTCA considers this to be a conformational fault (i.e., the terrier is not eligible for registration). There is really nothing that can be done to get the ears to fall to their normal position (i.e., folded over). Pay careful attention to the dam and sire of the puppy prior to purchase to see if your puppy may develop this condition. However it is important to remember that during the time period of 3 1/2 to 7 months of age, your Jack Russell is teething. During this time frame the ear set will do strange things, such as stand straight up, partially up and over to the side, etc. Don't panic, the ears may go back after the teething process is over. You should contact your breeder if the ears do not correct themselves after this time period.

Spots on Skin/Coat

A healthy Jack Russell has black or brown spots on their skin all over their entire body. When they are wet it is more noticeable. This is perfectly normal. The majority of Jack Russell Terriers have these skin spots. The spots will change in shade and size as your puppy matures. Your puppy may or may not develop "ticking." Ticking refers to small spots -- usually just a few hairs -- of color in the white coat. Ticking can be tan or black. Some dogs have both colors of ticking. It can be just a few spots or many, many spots. It changes with age as well. All remain at least 50% white. Some dogs may have no ticking at all in the first 14 weeks, and then begin to develop new "ticks" frequently with age. Ticking usually starts to appear at 7-8 months and will become thicker and more noticeable in the winter.

Brindle Markings

"Brindle" is a pattern of colors that is seen in the black, tan or brown colored area of the dog's coat. It should not be present in any white portions of the fur. It is a repeating, wavy, tiger-like pattern of black or tan within the colored areas. It's a sign of foreign blood in the dog's ancestry. For visual examples, look up pictures of Bull Terriers, Boxers, Great Danes and Mastiffs in a dog encyclopedia. It's an unregisterable color and therefore the dog should not be used for breeding. "Brindle" should not be confused with "grizzle" where black hairs are mixed with the tan.

Tail Docking on Jack Russell's

Jack Russell tails should be docked between 3-5 days of age. You should not dock the tails yourself unless you are a very experienced breeder. It is recommended that you take your pups to a licensed veterinarian to dock their tails. The formula for docking tails is: take 1/3 off, leave 2/3 on. If there are any doubts it is better to err on the side of too long than too short. You can always re-dock if the tail is too long but you can never add back on if docked too short. A common myth is that there is no such thing as a "standard length" of tail (i.e. 4"). The length of tail when the terrier reaches maturity will vary in relation to the size of the terrier. For example, a 10" terrier will have a shorter tail than a 15" terrier and vice versa. What is important is for the tail to be in balance with the overall size of the terrier. The tails are docked for reasons of tradition and hunting.

JRTCA (or other JRTC) Registrations

Unlike other registries which register entire litters at birth, each application for registration in the JRTCA is judged on the individual terrier's own merits; having registered parents will not guarantee that a pup can be registered. You must be a member of the JRTCA before your terrier can be registered. A terrier is not eligible for registration until it reaches one year of age and has attained its adult height, dentition, and other aspects considered for full maturity.

Registration Checklist
- Application
- JRTCA Membership
- Stud Certificate
- JRTCA Veterinarian Certificate
- Photographs
- Registration/Recording Fee
- Pedigree

Registration/Recording Fee
- $20 from JRTCA registered parents (both sire/dam)
- $35 from parents (one or both not registered with the JRTCA)
- $10 if terrier is spayed or neutered (recording only)

Club Policy/AKC/Recent Rule Changes

Assistants, volunteers and individual members do not make policies for the JRTCA and are often unable to answer specific questions or concerns. The JRTCA asks that you please direct questions/concerns about the AKC, JRTCA club policy and recent rule changes to the JRTCA Club office. You can contact the club office by email, phone, fax or postal mail (see below).

Jack Russell Terrier Club of America, Inc.
P.O. Box 4527
Lutherville, MD 21094-4527
Phone: (410) 561-3655
Fax: (410) 560-2563
eMail: JRTCA@worldnet.att.net

Chapter 5

How to show a Jack Russell

The most important issue to know is that Jack Russell's are first and foremost a working breed of Terrier. The emphasis is on the word "working" and that many Jack Russell enthusiasts find much more value on the Jack's work trials and attributes than in any type of dog showing competition. Some breeders will go as far as to say that if a Jack Russell is not used for field work than it's not a Jack Russell, but a misbreed that looks like a Jack Russell.

It's a good rule of thumb that if you do plan to enter your Jack in either showing or trial competitions that you should become very familiar with the breed standard. The standard can be found in Chapter 4 of this report. It's important to be honest with yourself about the breeding of your dog and its strengths and weaknesses according to the recognized standard. When you have a firm understanding of the standard and have reviewed the traits of your dog, if you decide to move ahead with competition, review the rules and regulations of your local or national Jack Russell Terrier Club or JRTC.

There is a very real danger to the survival of the Jack Russell caused by enthusiasts who breed the dog solely on appearance, only for showing events. Jack Russell's bred for looks and not with their original purpose eventually begin to lose the characteristics that make them a Jack Russell, and compromises that breeding line forever. The best breeding operations do their breeding with care towards the survival of the original Jack Russell. These programs focus on producing working Jack Russell Terriers and simply happen to show the ones that coincidentally meet the requirements for showing when one does.

Conformation or "showing" events are judged similar to any other dog pageant. The dog that wins is usually the contestant that most closely matches the official breed standard as it is recognized. Jack's entered into conformation events are judged on appearance, body movement, and temperament. In the case of the Jack Russell conformation is judged on the best mix of appearance and working characteristics. It's inevitable that working characteristics will play a role in conformation judging due to so much of the breed standard is based on what appear to be aesthetic appearances, but actually have a historical purpose in the use of hunting. Judges selected for Jack Russell conformation events are often required to meet specific standards. Selected judges for these events often have an intimate knowledge of the breed and have a pack of working Jack Russell's and the accompanying experience in field work with the animals. A judge must be aware of the work that the Jack Russell was bred to do.

Conformation showing of Jack Russell's has become increasingly popular in the U.S. This has been very effective in promoting the breeding of Jack Russell's that meet the conformation standard. In some ways this has helped to improve the genetics and breeding stock of the Jack Russell. It is however a delicate balance and breeders must be cautious to not spoil their line by getting caught up in breeding for appearance over function. Showing has been beneficial to the breed in the way of generating more public interest in the skills trial events as well, something that the JRTCA have strived to keep in the forefront as an example of where a Jack Russell's value truly lies.

Tips on Conformation Showing
- Train your dog well to be obedient on a leash and comfortable and social around strangers.
- The condition of your terrier plays an important role in how your terrier will be judged.
- When you are asked by a judge to walk your terrier, walk him. Set your sights on where you want to go and walk there, briskly. Do not hold the leash too tightly.
- Keep your attention on the judge. If the judge is busy you and your dog can relax. When the judge is looking in your direction make sure your dog is standing alertly.
- No matter what your terrier does when you are showing him. The change in his body language will affect his appearance.
- Make sure there is adequate space between your terrier and the ones on either side.
- Be a good sport. If you lose, be a good loser. If you win be a good winner. This means congratulating and thanking your competitors.

JRTCA Conformation Officials
- Judge - sanctioned by the JRTCA; judges terriers based upon JRTCA breed standard
- Apprentice Judge - may be in the conformation ring with the judge; learns how to judge terriers
- Ring Steward - verifies entries are correct; has ribbons and trophies ready for the judge
- Announcer - keeps exhibitors aware of class in progress and next class to show; announces class results
- Paddock Steward - usually at the gate and checks in the next class to go in the ring. It is a courtesy and makes the trial go more smoothly to let this person know you are ready for your class

Official JRTCA Rules
1. All terriers are to be judged on the JRTCA Breed Standard, unless otherwise noted.
2. Classes may be combined or split at the discretion of the Trial Chairperson, with the exception of Working Terrier classes, which may not be combined.
3. A terrier bred by a Sanctioned JRTCA Judge may not be shown under that Judge in the conformation division.
4. Only another exhibitor in that class, the Ring Steward or the Judge may make a question concerning the type of coat on any terrier. Requests for review of coat made by spectators will not be honored.
5. Spayed or neutered terriers may not compete in Puppy, Family, Open Adult, or Working Conformation. Spayed or neutered terriers may compete in the Miscellaneous Conformation section classes. Miscellaneous Conformation section classes are optional and offered at the discretion of the Trial Chairperson. When optional classes are offered, they must be judged by a JRTCA Sanctioned Judge and follow the JRTCA Sanctioned Trial rules.

6. No cross-entering within the Open Conformation and Working Conformation sections or between the Open and Working Conformation sections.
7. Exhibitors participating in the Working Classes must submit the appropriate JRTCA paperwork with entries. The Judge may require a copy of the Natural Hunting Certificate be presented to the Ring Steward at the time of judging.
8. Registered terriers may submit a copy of NHC Application, signed by a JRTCA Working Judge, within 30 days of the date it was issued.
9. Excessive use of squeaky or fur-like baiting devices by exhibitors is prohibited in the conformation ring. "Excessive use" will be at the Judge's discretion.
10. The only individuals permitted in the Conformation Ring, other than class participants, are the Judge, the Ring Steward, and, if asked for by the Judge or Ring Steward, the Trial Chairperson and Trial Photographer. Class participants include one handler per terrier. Terrier must be exhibited on lead.
11. A Child Handler class is offered for those children aged 5 through 9 years to have an introductory experience handling and learning about the Jack Russell Terrier. Terrier must be six months or older. Must be offered at all JRTCA Sanctioned Trials.

JRTCA Conformation Classes

The Conformation Division at a sanctioned trial consists of: Regular (Puppy, Open Adult, Working) and Miscellaneous.

4-6 Month Puppy
- Dog (smooth,rough/broken)
- Bitch (smooth,rough/broken)
- Best 4 up to 6 month Puppy and Reserve

6-12 Month Puppy
- Dog (6-9 months, 9-12 months, coat)
- Best Puppy Dog and Reserve
- Bitch (6-9 months, 9-12 months, coat)
- Best Puppy Bitch and Reserve
- Puppy Conformation Champion and Reserve

Open Adult
No cross-entering is permitted within the Open Division. Cross-entering is not permitted between the Open Division and the Working Division.
- Bred by Exhibitor Dog/Bitch (optional)
- American Bred Dog/Bitch (optional)
- Dogs (height, coat)
- Best Open Dog and Reserve
- Bitches (height, coat)
- Best Open Bitch and Reserve
- Best Open Terrier and Reserve

Working Terrier

Open to any JRTCA registered terrier owned by a JRTCA member which holds a JRTCA Natural Hunting Certificate. Terriers entering the Working Division may not cross-enter into the Open Division.

- Bronze Medallion Dogs and Bitches
- Working Terrier Dogs (may be separated by height, coat)
- Best JRTCA Working Terrier Dog and Reserve
- Working Terrier Bitches (height, coat)
- Best JRTCA Working Terrier Bitch and Reserve
- JRTCA Working Terrier Conformation Champion and Reserve

Family (Optional)

- **Stud Dog & Get**. Open to a sire with at least two, but not more than three offspring at parent's side. Judged on Breed Standard and consistency of type.
- **Brood Bitch & Produce**. Open to a dam with at least two, but not more than three offspring at parent's side. Judged on Breed Standard and consistency of type.
- **BEST FAMILY & RESERVE**. Open to 1st and 2nd place winners in above classes. No entry fee. "OPTIONAL"

Miscellaneous I - Youth Handler

- **Child Handler**. Open to any child aged 5 through 9 handling a Jack Russell Terrier. Judged on the child's knowledge of the Jack Russell and ability to present his or her dog. Quality of the dog NOT to be considered.
- **Junior Handler**. Open to any child aged 10 through 16 handling a Jack Russell Terrier. Judged on the child's knowledge of the Jack Russell and ability to present his or her dog. Quality of the dog NOT to be considered.

Miscellaneous II (Optional - Open to intact or spayed/neutered terriers)
Judged on JRTCA Breed Standard unless otherwise stated.

- **Novice**. Open to any adult Jack Russell which has never placed 1st through 4th in an adult regular or 1st in any Novice Conformation Class, at this or ANY prior sanctioned trial. "OPTIONAL"
- **Neutered Dog**. "OPTIONAL"
- **Spayed Bitch**. "OPTIONAL"
- **Veteran Terrier**. Open to any Jack Russell Terrier six years or older. Judged on the Breed Standard and condition of the dog. Entrants spayed or altered for health reasons not to be penalized. "OPTIONAL"
- **State or Region Bred**. Open to any adult Jack Russell Terrier bred in the State of _____. "OPTIONAL"
- **Suitability To Groundhog**. "OPTIONAL"
- **Suitability to Red Fox**. "OPTIONAL"
- **Suitability to Grey/Fox**. "OPTIONAL"
- **Suitability to Raccoon/Badger**. "OPTIONAL"

Jack Russell Trial Events

Terrier trials are a great chance for Jack Russell owners to meet and greet, and for their Jack Russell's to socialize and make friends. These events also give professional breeders a chance to see specimens from various breeding stock from around the world. This interaction is crucial in order for Jack Russell breeders and enthusiast to be able to continue promoting the improvement of Jack Russell bloodlines and breeding quality.

The JRTCA sanctions trials throughout the US. Other JRTC's will sanction events in their respective countries. The mandate of most JRTC's in sanctioning trial events is to ensure fair competition and the safety of the terriers. Human and canine participants of these events compete in Conformation, Go-to-Ground, Racing, Agility, Obedience, Youth Division and Trailing and Locating. The 2006 JRTCA trial events were held on October 19 - 21 at the Steppingstone Museum in the Susquehanna State Park, next to the Susquehanna River, in the state of Maryland. If you are interested in attending or participating in a JRTCA sanctioned trial, please view the www.terrier.com. Trial event locations and maps can be found at the site as well.

JRTCA Trial Rules

The JRTCA sanctions trials throughout the US to ensure a fair and standardized competition and the safety of exhibitors and terriers. Trial rules have been established over many years, with the input of many people, both trial chairpersons and exhibitors alike. They are designed to ensure the integrity and consistency of sanctioned trials. The JRTCA Rule Book was designed to assist JRTCA members to better understand what to expect at a sanctioned trial and the rules governing the actual running of the trial. It is an attempt to enable every trial to run smoothly and be an enjoyable experience for everyone. You can access the JRTCA sanctioned trial rules when you are away from your computer by using a web-enabled phone. To use this feature, point the browser on your cell phone to www.terrier.com/rules. You will be able to browse the current general and event-specific rules.

JRTCA Sanctioned Events

Conformation

Conformation classes are judged much like any other dog show. The winner is the dog that most closely matches the breed standard. In addition to conformation and movement, the dog is judged on temperament; as in all things having to do with Jack Russell's the best working dog is being sought.

Racing

Racing is perhaps the most exciting of all the terrier trial events. A sanctioned track is a straight course with a starting box at one end and a stack of straw bales at the other. A lure is attached to a string that is pulled along by a generator. The dogs are muzzled for safety. The first dog through the hole in the straw bales is the winner.

Go-To-Ground

Go-to-ground is an event that simulates a hunting situation. The terrier traverses a tunnel and attempts to find a quarry at the end of the tunnel. The tunnel has several turns to make it harder for the terrier. The terrier with the fastest time to the quarry is considered the winner. The terrier must mark (i.e., bark, scratch, whine) to qualify the time.

Agility

Agility is a trial event in which dogs traverse a maze of obstacles and compete for speed and accuracy. Terriers jump through tires, zip through tunnels, scale a 5'7" A-Frame, traverse a narrow "dog walk", negotiate a see-saw, zigzag through closely spaced, upright poles and soar over a variety of challenging hurdles. The sport has an overwhelming spectator appeal, largely because of the fast pace, the challenging and visually appealing obstacles and the contagious enthusiasm displayed by the dogs.

Obedience

Obedience involves both terrier and handler. Handler and terrier are required to perform a series of exercises that test the obedience of the terrier. Each exercise is graded by the obedience judge. Points may be subtracted for minor and substantial faults.

Youth

Youth competitors are expected to be on time, neat and workman-like, listen to and follow directions and show a genuine effort to communicate and work with their terrier. There is a great need to offer things for our youth to do with their terriers, particularly as it also provides a chance to learn

Trailing and Locating

Trailing and locating events involve the terrier tracking and locating a quarry (above ground). The terrier is judged on his ability to follow a line in a simulated natural hunting environment, to locate, mark and open on the quarry. The terrier is judged on a combination of time and accuracy. The terrier with the fastest time is not necessarily the winner.

Non-Sanctioned Events

Many trials offer fun events for all terriers. These events are for the fun and enjoyment of the dogs and their owners and will vary from one event to the other. Non-sanctioned events can include such activities as: High Jump, Field Luring Courses, Timed Individual Racing, Weenie Bobbing and Retrieving, Muskrat Swimming Races, and more. Ask your regional JRTC about what non-sanctioned events that they offer or at the registration desk of any official event you are attending.

Working the Jack Russell Terrier

The Jack Russell is named after the famous English reverend that created the breed in the mid 1800's. He bred the Jack on his homestead in Devonshire, England with only one purpose in mind; fox hunting. In the Jack, the Reverend sought to create the greatest hunting terrier known to man. Many would say that he succeeded.

The reason that the Jack Russell survives today and has avoided the drastic changes that have occurred in breeds such as its cousin, the Fox Terrier, is because those who enjoy the Jack Russell believed in the reverend's vision and made every effort to breed the Jack in a way that would preserve its characteristics as a working dog. These dedicated enthusiasts have maintained the quality of the Jack Russell, including the Reverend himself, for nearly 200 years.

Organizations such as the JRTCA prize the working quality of the Jack Russell above all else. Everything bred into the Jack Russell is related directly to its usefulness in fox hunting. The coloring, conformation, character, and intelligence of the Jack Russell make it an ideal hunter of small game. A healthy working Jack should be compact, have balanced proportions, the legs straight, and the chest must be small enough to enter a fox den without problems. The Jack Russell is extremely flexible, which allows him to chase his prey even in its own underground tunnels. These characteristics are necessary for the Jack to be a successful hunter. Wherever a fox goes a Jack Russell must be able to follow. The Jack Russell is also ideal for hunting groundhog, raccoon and other wild game.

Jack Russell's are bred to be fearless and chase a fox into its dark underground tunnels without hesitation hot on its heels. A good Jack will bark at a cornered prey even underground and will not budge unless its enemy escapes through another tunnel or it's called out. It's important that a Jack Russell does not kill a fox on site, but only confines it until the huntsman arrives. One story says that a pair of Jack Russell's was feared lost and dead after chasing a raccoon into an abandoned fox den. The owners were very fond of the pets and desired to recover their remains in order for proper burial. Twelve hours after entering the hole, diggers, and machinery were brought in to find the remains. Instead they found the pair alive and well inside of a buried unused culvert, with the raccoon they chased still cornered at the back of the pipe.

Legendary hunting tales have even been told of the Jack Russell being able to stay cornering prey underground for days or more without food or water because of their strong hunting bred instincts. It is cautioned that inexperienced hunters with inexperienced dogs should not take their Jack's out on unplanned hunting excursions for fun or on a whim. Although the Jack is known as a formidable fighter, such activities being undertaken by the inexperienced can result in tragedy. Smart hunting can prevent the tragedy of injury or death to a Jack in the form of animal attacks or the actions of panicking, inexperienced owners.

Chapter 6

Grooming and caring for the Jack Russell

There is a false myth that has been spread about the public that Jack Russell Terriers do not shed. The reality of this is that Jack Russell's do shed. A Jack Russell actually sheds more than a number of other breeds. Unlike most breeds it seems that the shorter the hair, the more it will shed, however there are exceptions and you may find your long haired rough coat shedding just as much a s the smooth coated version. The shedding may get worse as the seasons change. Excessive bathing will also cause excessive shedding, and possibly even skin problems. It's recommended that you do some research and do not bathe your dog any more than is necessary.

A JRT owner was once overheard saying, "*The coat type you choose is all determined by what length of white hair you wish to vacuum.*" If shedding was a sport than the Jack Russell would be a much a master of it is it as at hunting. This is not a good breed for homes with people who have allergies or are looking for a low-shedding pet.

Shedding Tips

Brushing with a brush or a rubber mitt helps lessen the amount you have to vacuum up by catching it before it ends up on your furniture.

- Experiment with using a soft rubber horse curry for grooming. You may find that the curry not only removes loose hair, but your Jack Russell may enjoy the massage like experience as well. A horse curry may also work for getting hair out of upholstery.
- Try brushing most of the upper body toward the base of the tail, then grab a "swiffer" sheet and rub it down his back, trying to collect all of the loose hair at the base of his tail in one swoop.
- Don't over bathe your dog, and when you do bathe him don't use shampoos etc. unless he really needs it. A good warm water rinse is often enough.

When traveling with your Jack Russell be sure to make sure your travel arrangement are all well thought out well ahead of time, with an emphasis on comfort and safety for your pet. If traveling by air, be aware that each airline has different rules/regulations regarding air travel for pets. In extremely hot times of the year or in certain destinations pet travel may be prohibited or restricted due to the heat. There also may be restrictions on size, and as much as you'd like to have it travel with you it may have to travel as cargo. Please do your research before you travel with your Jack. There are also steps and safety tips that you should follow when traveling. Try to make sure you take your Jack Russell inside the cabin with you when traveling. You will have to make arrangements in advance with the airlines and may want to discuss some ideas and the unique needs of your pet with the airline; they may think of ideas or concerns that you haven't thought of.

Grooming

Very few animals in the dog showing circuit appear exactly as they were meant to naturally when on the show room floor. If you do decide to show your Jack Russell Terrier it's no exception. The Jack Russell can benefit from some intensive grooming before arriving at a dog show. The Jack Russell is one of the few remaining breeds still capable of earth work, and as such, his coat is very important to the job he is bred for. A healthy Jack Russell's coat is hard, dense and lies close to the body. In preparing your Jack Russell for a show, remember that the breed standard specifies, *smooth without being sparse, so as to protect from the elements and undergrowth*. In order keep your Jack's coat in good condition, the coat should be plucked or stripped at least six to eight weeks prior to the show. Plucking involves using a stripping knife, a course knife for the body, medium knife for the neck and shoulders, and a fine blade for head and ears. Ask your local pet supply specialist about the different types, how to use them, etc. For those who are unfamiliar with the stripping process, the knife is grasped in the right hand, taking a few hairs between the thumb and knife blade, and giving a sharp pull. Dogs that have never been stripped before will be uneasy the first few times. For dog's new to the process it is advised to do a little at a time over a longer period, so they can adjust. The knife should be held parallel to the dog's body to avoid leaving chop marks in the coat.

Speak to your dog while grooming in a soothing, reassuring tone. If you don't say anything while just pulling hair, he will get bored and start moving around. If the dog resists grooming in one area, move to another; you can always go back. As your dog becomes more accustomed to this grooming try to develop your own system to follow for grooming so that the dog has a consistent experience. First, brush or comb the entire dog. Then, begin grooming at the head and work your way down his body, leaving the sensitive areas such as the belly, anal area, and penile sheath or nipples until last. When the dog has learned to trust you, he will be less nervous. If the dog gets fidgety, move to another area. To groom the face you need to pull the skin taut, firmly grasp a few adjoining hairs between your thumb and forefinger and pull in the direction of growth.

Toe nails need to be trimmed back often, especially on non-working Jack's, but carefully. You can purchase special dog toe nail clippers from your local pet store. Be very careful not to cut through the nail quick. Removing a small amount of nail, you will see a small white dot in the center. As you remove more nail, you'll see a red dot that is the beginning of the quick, which is the blood supply to the nail. Stop at this point. If you accidentally cut the quick the bleeding can be stopped with nail clotting powder. You can purchase this from your veterinarian. Corn starch or some cotton applied with pressure to the end of the nail may work as well. After the toe nails have been trimmed, use a small sharp scissor to trim and round the hair of the feet and trim the long hairs between the toe pads.

Grooming Rough and Broken Coated Jack Russell's

Grooming a rough or broken coated terrier for life at home is much easier than grooming them for show. For home life all that is really needed is a good combing with a slicker brush once in a while to remove dirt and loose hair. You can trim the coat with a basic pair of electric clippers as well in order to keep the fur at a manageable length. It's important to note that it is not advised to trim a rough coat Jack Russell with electric clippers for show, only for dogs who simply live in a home and do not compete in showing events. This is because clippers do not create proper coat texture needed that is a requirement in showing events. Trimming with clippers can cause the dogs fur to start curling as it grows. For better results for a showing dog it is recommended to use a Dresser comb, available at local pet stores. On an older Jack, it's advised to forgo the stripping blade process and simply brush.

Rough and broken coated Jack Russell's are groomed for three basic reasons: appearance, comfort, and most importantly, to help the dog continue to develop a good hard coat that will repel water. Ideally, grooming is done no less than twice a year. An early grooming in February will have your dog's coat in good condition by late March or April and will keep him more comfortable in summer. If your Jack is a show dog, his coat will be back to normal before the trial season begins. Groom again in late August in order to keep the coat in good condition for the fall. The dog will have a full coat for winter. No dog should be groomed prior to or at a trial event. Some competitors have tried to whiten the coats of their Jack Russell's with the use of chalk. This practice, or the use of any other substance, is strictly frowned upon.

How to Groom

Many owners do not believe in cutting the hair but, rather, pluck or pull it. If you simply cut the hair off, dead hair shafts remain in the skin. Nature will push them out eventually, but in the meantime, new growth will be uneven and the dog will always look unkempt. Give the dog a complete brush to start then carefully separate the long hairs by combing or brushing in small sections. Pluck or pull only a few hairs at a time, you'll remove the dead hair and new growth will be even. Moreover, the new hairs will be coarser. Once he is used to it your dog will not mind being groomed at all. Remember to talk in a positive, reassuring tone while grooming.

Equipment

There is no set of strict of rules to use for combing. If a certain comb seems to work well for you, use it. A good grooming kit to have in case you need it is; a wide-toothed comb, wire brush, a short serrated knife with a dull blade, a short serrated knife with a sharp blade and a pair of thinning shears. Make sure you provide the dog with a good stable footing to stand on. If you have him on a tabletop or slippery floor, be sure to stand him in a way that has a good grip. Always begin with a general brushing and then work from the face to the tail.

The Sides

There is nothing wrong with leaving a few whiskers around the eyes and mouth. You want the dog to look neat, clean, defined and trimmed, but not bald. When you reach the fine white undercoat of the fur do not groom any further. When you touch the coat you should feel the softer undercoat underneath. As the hair grows you should actually be able to feel the rougher surface coat emerging as it grows.

The Neck

Keep the neck skin taut in the area where you are grooming. Begin at the back of the neck and work around to the front. The hair is likely to go wild around the cowlicks. Pull the skin back in small areas and pluck a few hairs at a time, working around the cowlick. When the head and neck are plucked, you may want to take the sharper knife and gently, barely touching the fur, comb in the directions of hair growth. You want to remove only the long hair.

The Chest

Brush the hair away from its direction of growth so you can see where it is, then pull toward the direction of growth, keeping the skin underneath taut.

Legs

The bumps on the knees of rough and broken-coated Jack Russell's are usually just hair. In most cases the bumps will disappear as you groom. Groom the back legs also; you want to see the lines of the stifle. Don't forget to show the feet. The dog won't like it, so you may have to go back and forth to them between grooming other parts. It's perfectly fine to trim the hair between the toes with scissors.

Legs and Back

Using scissors to trim the entire coat of the dog is not recommended and will present future problems with the coat. Take the time to pluck the hair. Dogs mind having the shoulders and back done less than almost any other part of their body. Take your time; comb or brush the hair away from the direction of growth, grasp a few long hairs, tighten the skin, and pull in the direction of growth.

A little gentle plucking around the anal area is also important. Long hairs tend to get dirty and make the dog uncomfortable. Gentle use of the dull knife will preserve the cowlicks, but get rid of excess hair. Make the skin taut by pulling up on the dog's tail.

Use scissors to trim around the penile sheath, and remove the urine-soaked hair. If you are not experienced, you may want to ask someone to hold your dog for you at this time. The same applies for the area around the nipples, before she whelps. It's not uncommon to see rough-coated bitches groom prior to whelping, by pulling the hair with their teeth; you can be a real help to her by doing it for her.

The Tail

Pull long hair the length of the tail. It is acceptable to use thinning scissors to trim the long hair at the tip of the tail area. After you've groomed the long hairs from the rest of the tail, hold the tip and clip the few extra long hairs to make the end of the tail tidy.

The Final Steps

When you are done; closely inspect the final appearance of your dog. You will likely have to go back and redo some areas to get stray hairs that you have missed. This is also the time to go over your dog with the dull stripping knife. It's very important to be careful when grooming with a stripping knife along the backbone. It is very easy to skin and nick areas on the spine along the vertebrae; this is caused by careless grooming.

The End Result

At the beginning, always take your time learning and getting your dog used to grooming. Split it into as many sessions as you need, and take as much time as necessary. The grooming speed will increase as you and your dog both become accustomed with the process. Continue to try and accomplish more and perform longer sessions each time until you can finally achieve it all in one session. Grooming is a very good form of discipline training for your dog.

Some Afterthoughts

Inspect your dogs coat again 4-7 days after grooming. If you discover hair that has turned yellow, this is hair that was loosened by grooming and has now died. You will also likely find hair that has grown out enough again. Give the dog another quick groom and it will help preserve a healthy, water resistant coat. Grooming is also a good time to inspect the good health of your dog's ears, teeth and eyes. Clean these areas where necessary. If you see mikes, strange symptoms, or foul odor from the ears consult your veterinarian. This is also a good time to ensure that the dog's anal glands are well drained.

If you are unsure how to do this schedule an appointment with your vet. Grooming is a good time to weigh your dog. Fluctuations or increases in weight may be a sign that a change in diet is needed. Checking your dog's nails and trimming if necessary is advised. Make sure that you do check your dog's nails often, not just when grooming.

If your dog has fleas, use a flea powder or spray. Some owners avoid bathing their dogs. They are often out in the rain which helps clean them, but good grooming results in a coat that sheds dirt; good grooming is more important than bathing. If bathing is absolutely necessary, do so at least two weeks before you show the dog to give his coat a chance to recover. Water is not detrimental to a Jack Russell Terrier's coat, but shampoo is. Cornstarch mixed with baby powder in equal parts makes a good dry shampoo. Work the powder into the coat and, using a brush, remove it. Be sure to remove all of the powder.

Check your dog's neck often to be sure that their collar is loose enough that it's not chaffing the skin, but tight enough that he will not slip out. Don't leave hard plastic collars such as anti-bark and invisible fence collars on at all times; they can seriously damage the skin. Flat collars can also damage the skin. It is recommended to use rolled collars of leather or nylon.

Food for your Jack Russell

Diet is extremely important for every pet. It's recommended that you feed your Jack Russell a premium dog food that uses human grade ingredients, not loaded with grains and chemical preservatives. Many lower quality foods will contain split grains. You'll see Chicken, Lamb, etc., but also several different types of corn or other grain that will outweigh the meat, making the food grain-based. Dogs are carnivores that can live well on an omnivorous diet, but should still be feed a predominantly meat based food whenever possible. Stay away from chemical preservatives such as BHA, BHT and Ethoxyquin. When feeding canned food, find a high quality canned food. Most of the premium foods also sell a canned food.

Never feed your dog cooked bones. Cooked bones will splinter and can cause serious or fatal injury. Give raw marrow bones of the appropriate size. Jack Russell's have been known to get their lower jaw stuck in the middle of a large bone. Make sure the bones you give them are small enough that this doesn't happen, but large enough that your dog does not swallow them whole and choke on them.

Some pet owners swear by the "BARF" diet, which is bones and raw food. For information on feeding a raw diet, there are several books that you can look for by authors such as Dr. Richard Pitcairn, Ian Billinghurst and Kymythy Shultze. You can also search online for more information on the BARF diet and home cooked diets. Please be sure to get one of the books. Although many dogs do very well on these diets, they need to be feed in the proper way or other serious health issues may result.

There is no specific amount to feed your Jack Russell, and the amount of food needed will change with things like age, climate and exercise. You should be able to feel the ribs, but not see them. As a general guideline, a healthy Jack Russell should weigh 1 to 1.25 lbs per inch of length.

Electronic Fences

There are a variety of professional and personal opinions regarding the use of electronic fences for Jack Russell's. Opinions run the entire range of for, against and neutral. The best method of making such a decision is to do all of your research and determine your own personal decisions on the idea in order to make the decision that's right for you. There are a number of companies, assistants, and informational resources that can help you make a decision about whether an electronic fence is right for you and your Jack.

Whether you agree with the idea of an electronic fence or not, is should be stressed that Jack Russell Terriers absolutely need containment! They will roam due to their hunting instincts even if left in an unsecured area for only a few minutes. You can let them out every day for three years with no trouble, but one day they will disappear and may never come back. Many Jack's are killed by cars when darting across the road after a squirrel or a cat. Even the most intelligent, well trained, road savvy Jack will forget about the danger when there is game afoot.

In some instances it may be impractical to secure your Jack Russell with a physical fence, such as zoning regulations, size of property, etc. In these cases, you should find an alternate form of pet containment. This brings about the consideration of electronic pet containment. There is no clear consensus on the usefulness or efficacy of electronic pet containment systems. Some owners have had bad experiences with them and lost pets while others have had great success. It's difficult to determine whether these experiences are a result of the brand of pet containment, the personality of the terrier, the diligence of the owner, the obedience of the terrier, good/bad luck, proper installation, or other pet/animal factors

Reasons for electronic pet containment systems:
- Effective if properly designed, installed and maintained.
- Invisible - cannot be seen to detract from beauty of property.
- Can keep dogs out of gardens, pools, etc.
- Can be used to prevent digging under or climbing over regular fencing.

Reasons against electronic pet containment systems:
- Does not keep other animals from entering the yard.
- A feisty enough terrier will take the hit from the fence if he really wants what is beyond its boundary.
- Some feel that the jolt that the pet gets when crossing the electric fence is inhumane.

Other opinions:
- If you decide to use an electronic pet containment system, make sure that it is properly designed, installed and maintained.
- Teach your terrier basic obedience, in conjunction with the use of an electronic system.
- Watch your dog while they are outside no matter what kind of containment you have in place

The bottom line: do what you think is right for you and your Jack. It's up to you to make an informed decision on whether or not to use this kind of containment system. For more help and questions you can contact one of the following pet containment specialists:

- Bob Franklin (farmcliff@home.com)
- Linda Cranford (workjrs@vnet.net)
- Diana Hufnagel (dbHuf@aol.com)
- Meredith Jarman (meredith@lynxus.com)
- Judy Churchfield (judyc@greenapple.com)
- Heather Reid (jrtrescue@spectrumanalytic.com)

Toys

The type of toys you purchase will depend greatly on your individual dog. Experiment and buy your Jack Russell the kinds of toys he seems to like and enjoy most. Some dogs love squeaky toys, some destroy them. The same can be said of any other toy. Do not leave your dog unattended with any kind of toy, especially for long periods of time. Many Jacks are very rough on toys and destroy them. Small pieces can become lodged in their throat or digestive tract and health concerns.

Many people will give their Jack's pig ears and hooves. Others don't feel comfortable feeding them due to the risk of choking, and the possibility of chemicals used in the process of making them. Raw marrow bones are great for chewing, but supervision is recommended. Some dogs will get an upset stomach from the marrow. You can scoop it out before giving them to the dogs. Also, be sure the hollow middle part of the bone is small enough or large enough that the dogs jaw cannot get stuck in between and that the bone is large enough not to be swallowed and present a choking hazard.

Kong toys are quite popular and can be filled with treats, peanut butter, a spray flavoring available at your pet store, even yogurt or Jell-O. Most dogs enjoy the challenge of getting what's in the middle. Many dogs will gravitate towards plush toys and rope bones. If your dog has a very intelligent or curious personality keep them busy with a treat dispenser or treat dispensing toy that they have to work at and figure out in order to get treats. Edible artificial bones can be a good toy or treat as well. Experts suggest not using bones that contain plastic and chemical preservatives. All toys, not matter how unassuming or non-threatening they appear can present a risk. Always supervise your dog.

Rescue, Adoption, and Other Issues

Most Jack Russell rescue organizations cannot place a dog that is aggressive to humans. Dogs that are terminally ill are also often not accepted by rescue groups as they are also not suitable for adoption. Rescue shelters are not a clearing house for dogs with serious behavior or health problems. Many groups will assist or council an owner in need of advice and try to help find ways to keep a dog in its current home.

It is not considered acceptable practice to use a rescue dog for breeding. Many rescue operations will stipulate that all dogs must be spayed or neutered as part of the adoption process, and are meant strictly as pets. Many of the dogs rescued are not good examples of the breed standard, and often there is no pedigree or record of ancestry.

Surrender charges for relinquishing a dog will vary from group to group. Some groups do not charge, some do. Most groups require relinquishing owners to be responsible for having the dog's medical requirements up-to-date, including spaying or neutering, and a current health record. Many groups, those who charge and those who do not, encourage donations to help assist in the expenses involved in the dog's temporary care.

There is almost certainly a charge for adopting a dog. Some groups have an official adoption rate, some ask for a general donation. These charges are necessary in order to cover the costs of care and preparing a dog for its new home. Some frequent costs are: travel expenses, travel crates, spaying/neutering, vaccinations, veterinarian attention, etc. If there have been no expenses or costs, the dog is neutered/spayed, vaccinated, comes with leash, collar, bed etc. then the rescue group may offer a reduced rate on the dog. The average minimum adoption fee seems to be around $50.00. If there are specific, exorbitant costs relating to a dog such as travel, medical, etc. then the rescue group may ask that additional fees and expenses be covered for adoption. Remember, financial responsibilities do not stop after you adopt a dog. You will have to be accountable for yearly vaccinations, licensing etc. Be prepared for a lifetime of commitment.

Most rescue groups will screen applicants for pet adoption to ensure that they can provide a proper caring home and stable environment. In most cases approval is based on the understanding and acceptance of the nature of the terrier, the owners' lifestyle and their ability to house the dog properly. A fenced yard or invisible fence is required; the dog cannot be allowed to run free without supervision. Once a prospective owner is approved, the Rescue network then will try to match them up with the appropriate dog.

Many of the terriers needing homes are males ranging in ages one to four. Many people specifically seek out females for adopting because they are perceived as less aggressive and more affectionate. This is a misconception. Male Jack Russell's are as affectionate and loving as females. Since all rescue groups require animals to be neutered as part of the placement process, the gender should not matter. Males who are rejected by their original owners are often those nearing sexual maturity, and instead of neutering the dog, the owner puts them up for adoption. Often a male is rejected because of problems that can be resolved by neutering. Rescue group volunteers will often work to adjust behavior problems that are not serious in nature while the dog is in the shelter. Sometimes all that is needed is a telephone call to your local rescue agency to get tips on behavior training to avoid relinquishing your dog as a problem dog.

Are general shelters and humane societies helpful with Jack Russell rescue efforts? Some are great; others are not at all interested rescue groups, and are perhaps overprotective of their place in the industry. Often general animal shelters do not know that the dog in their care is of the Jack Russell breed and do not understand the dogs unique needs and personality.

How can you help lessen the number of Jack Russell's in need of rescue? Do not buy a Jack Russell from a pet store. Do not sell a Jack Russell to a pet store. Pet stores are fine for pet supplies but not the best place to purchase a puppy. Most pet stores do not screen those who buy their dogs, and only require that the person has the money to pay whatever they are charging. Many pet stores will overprice Jack Russell's and charge more than a recognized breeder. Do not sell a pup to someone who has not researched and understanding of what to expect. If you think the home is inappropriate do not sell to that person. Do the people have children? Do the children mind the adults? If they cannot control their children, they will for sure have problems with the dog.

A good breeding strategy is to have a very well laid out plan. Have screened homes picked out before breeding. If you do not have enough pre-approved buyers waiting for pups, do not breed. Be honest with potential buyers about the characteristics of the breed. If you do not have a serious breeding program, do not breed. Do not breed because you think it will be good for the health of your existing pet. There are too many unwanted pets, and certainly too few suitable homes for this special dog. Be responsible. If you are not breeding in order to contribute to and improve the breed than don't bother breeding. Leave it to the professionals. If breeding is beyond your time and ability you can always contribute by educating others about the unique personality and needs of the dog and that just because the Jack Russell is cute does not mean that it will fit every person's lifestyle.

Chapter 7

Breeding Jack Russell Terriers

The administrators of any good Jack Russell breeding program will focus on three major factors: The natural ability to hunt, temperament and conformation. Alongside the natural ability to hunt, breeders have found that size is an important criterion. The quarry that the dogs have to work is not large and in order to be able to succeed they have to able to maneuver in equally as small an area. Therefore breeders strive to breed terriers that will be under 12 ½" in length. It should be noted that Terriers over that size often have no trouble performing their tasks, but the smaller size is more desirable and is a better guarantee of good performance. Many breeders will seek out Jacks that have a unique split personality; an excellent hunter in the field and a docile affectionate nature in the home. The breeding of Jack's with this type of personality is encouraged. Conformation to Breed Standard revolves around a working dog. Form follows function. The Jack Russell Terrier Clubs have had the good sense to recognize that and have allowed for a breed standard to include a wide size range of Terriers.

Breeders and Puppies

Most Jack Russell Terrier clubs will not recommend specific breeders. If you are looking for a puppy, the best place to start is to contact your local club for an information pack or advice on what to look for. In the U.S. you can send for the JRTCA's information packet. In addition to breed and club information, this packet contains directory of breeders with listings from all over the U.S. Each breeder listing includes the basic details on that specific breeding operation; all breeders are current JRTCA members, and follow the current official Breeders Code of Ethics. The packet also contains a list of JRTCA state representatives and locally organized clubs which are affiliated with the JRTCA.

The packet may be obtained by sending $10 to:
JRTCA
P.O. Box 4527
Lutherville, MD 21094

Breeding

Before you begin breeding any dog, ask yourself "Why?" Why do you want to breed this dog? There are less than handful of good reasons and an extensive list of bad ones.

The Bad Reasons

Love

Breeding your female Jack out of love is not a good reason, no matter how good your intentions. No matter how routine, the birthing process for dogs is always a dangerous one, especially for smaller breeds. It has been known to happen more than people like to talk about for an adult female to die during birth, usually taking the pups with her either immediately or by way of any survivors not having a mother to care for them in the early days of life. If you read the book "Canine Reproduction" you'll notice that there are 54 pages on what can go wrong, and only one page on what it's like if everything goes well. The risks are very real, and even if everything goes well initially, there are defects that can show up later, causing the eventual death of the puppies.

Money

If you're breeding for money, you stand to lose a bundle. There are many minor defects that won't affect the puppy's chance for a happy life, but will cause a financial loss to the breeder, as a refund or replacement will need to be given to the buyer. Some of these defects may not show up until the puppy is into its first six months. Today Jack Russell Terriers are hot. Tomorrow, who are truly devoted to the breed will be paying the price for this surge in popularity with greatly increased use of rescue agencies as much of America finds out that Jack Russell's are a bit more dog than they want to handle. Right now, people aren't thinking about the future, and many novice breeders are anxious to try to supply the demand for puppies that the public currently has. A recent first time breeder was so impressed with the ease of selling her first litter, that she has purchased two more bitches with intent to breed. It's true, if you had two dozen puppies, you could sell them all in a weekend, if you weren't particular about who bought them. The novice breeder is blissfully ignorant of the fact that she may find half the litter dumped on her doorstep in a few months if she's not careful about who the puppies are sold to. If you think that your Jack Russell Terrier bitch is going to be a cash cow for you, you are in for quite a disappointment.

Because you want your kids to witness a birth and grow up with puppies

If you want them to watch a litter being born, call a breeder and see if you can make a deal to have them let you know when their next little is being born. Most children, and some adults, are repulsed by the gory parts of the whelping process, and will be disgusted by the miracle of nature you so hoped for them to enjoy. A litter growing up is often too rowdy for most small children. Very small children often end up terrified of the leaping creatures with sharp nails and teeth.

Because you love your dog so much that you want another one just like her

The chances that you'll get one "just like her" are almost non-existent. Just because your dog is beautiful and perfect does not mean that her offspring will be.

Because everyone who visits says they'd love to have a puppy from her

First of all, some of your friends are just trying to be polite. When a litter actually arrives, even a planned one, many prospective buyers change their minds and offer a number of excuses. Many people get left holding the bag with a little of five or more pups as people back out of the commitment with reasons like:
"The kids aren't old enough yet."
"The kids are too old now to be bothered taking care of a dog."
"We're going to have a baby."
"We'll be moving in 3 months -- wait till then."
"The rug is too new."

Because you love having little puppies

If you are not an experienced breeder and have never had to care for an entire litter of Jack Russell pups, your opinion of them may soon change. Having a pack of baby Jack Russell's can cause a number of problems in your home such as the mess a litter makes. Can you put up with the cleaning that is constantly involved in caring for a litter? There's no way to explain how tired you'll get of scrubbing up after the puppies, their whelping box, the yard, the kennel, or wherever they're kept. They dump their food and water the minute you put it down, step in it, roll in it, and drag it through whatever else may be in the puppy box. With 4 or 5 puppies, there's always something else to be cleaned up, too! The responsibility you'll have with a litter, it's not as easy as having the bitch whelp the litter and takes care of them until they're ready to go. Much of it is up to you, and you're tied to the litter like any new mother.

More Questions and Information on Breeding

Weigh the positives and the negatives carefully before you decide to breed. If you're an amateur, get the advice of a good veterinarian before you do anything! Now that you've some idea of what's involved with raising a litter, there are still plenty of other things to be considered. Is your bitch breeding quality? Is she JRTCA approved? Always register your bitch before breeding. To not do so is much like locking the barn door after the horse has escaped. Do you know her faults as well as her virtues? Is she of desirable temperament? Are you prepared for the difficulty of placing Jack Russell puppies? Are you prepared to keep them as long as necessary - maybe even 4-6 months? Do you think you can make money raising Jack Russell Terriers?

Before you breed there's a few things that should be done to prevent trouble. These things will add to the expense of breeding a litter, but are very necessary. A prospective brood bitch should be in top physical condition. An overweight bitch lacking in exercise tolerance may have trouble whelping. If your bitch isn't in top shape, skip the next heat and get her in shape before you breed. Once you decide to breed, take her to your veterinarian for a physical check up before she comes in heat. This is a good time to have her registration exam done, if you haven't already done it. Her physical exam should also include a test for heartworms in areas where this is a problem. She should be given all her booster shots at this time too. Because of an increase in the incidence of brucellosis in dogs, a serum agglutination test should be done before mating. This test is available in veterinary clinics and can be run from a blood sample in minutes. Also, before mating, the bitch should be checked for worms. Round worms are difficult to avoid in puppies. Other parasites should also be vigorously treated. A bitch with an active parasite infestation is less likely to whelp healthy puppies.

Before she comes in season is the time to find a stud dog that will enhance your bitch. Get several breeders' opinions of a good choice for a stud dog. If they only recommend dogs owned by them, take their opinion with a grain of salt. They may be speaking out of greed rather than a sincere desire to match with the right stud. Once you've narrowed down the field of prospective mates, study their genetic backgrounds. Even if the dog looks perfect, he may be hiding many genetic faults. Study the background of both your bitch and the prospective stud and make an educated decision based on conformation, pedigree, working ability, and temperament. This will help you increase the odds of getting a healthy litter. Once your bitch comes in season, you'll need to contact the stud owner, and you'll be advised when to bring your dog to him. Plan to pay the stud fee at that time. You may also be charged for boarding if your bitch is to stay with the stud dog's owner. The suitable stud for your bitch may be some distance away, necessitating additional travel expense.

Now you have approximately 62 days to worry, get your wits about you, and get ready for the big event. Even if the breeding and pregnancy go smoothly, the pet owner will likely run into problems with the delivery. Many times these problems are not real, but result from a lack of experience on the part of the owner. The first time, an amateur breeder either rushes to the vet at the first signs of labor, or fails to recognize when the dog is having serious problems and does not seek help in time to save the pups and the mother. Either way, this lack of experience can cost a lot of money. Even if all goes smoothly, and the bitch produces a nice litter of puppies, the chances of further problems and complications increase from this point on. She may not be an adequate mother. She may neglect her puppies or even kill them, have no milk, have a post delivery infection, or the puppies may be weak or get sick. If your bitch can't or won't take care of her puppies, guess who'll have to do it?

Every two hour tube feedings and messy cleanups are just a few of the joys of breeding. Then the pups have to be cared for, weaned, fed, cleaned, vaccinated and wormed. All time consuming jobs, and additional expense. It is most often the experience of amateur breeders that when they add up their out-of-pocket expenses and deduct the money received from sales, the result will be negative; without even counting the labor they've invested. A year from now you may get a call from the purchaser of one of the puppies to tell you that the puppy has a genetic defect that has just shown up. Now you'll have to refund part of the money they paid for the pup. You could be paying for the privilege of breeding for months or years to come.

There are a number of reasons to consider spaying your bitch instead of breeding her. We've all seen the news, where in hopes of shocking the general public into awareness of the pet population problem they film employees of the animal shelter putting a beautiful dog to sleep. This problem is all too common with the Jack Russell.

Talk to anyone involved in performing Jack Russell rescue and they will tell you that the problem is growing to the point that it's becoming overwhelming. Many rescue facilities have a strong staff that goes far beyond the call of duty to rescue dogs from the pounds and neglectful owners each year. As many as been rescued, even more slip through the cracks. Many animal shelter employees don't recognize what a Jack Russell looks like, and so they don't inform the proper rescue groups. Some day the dog you see on T.V. being put to sleep may be a Jack Russell. Is it one of the pups you bred?

No dog should have to pay for your mistakes or learning experience with its life. If you can't afford to take care of an animal for the rest of its life, think seriously about spaying your female or not owning pets at all. It's simple and cost effective. The money you'll save on the licensing fee alone will probably pay for the operation in just a few years. A spayed bitch is also less likely to roam, be more sociable with other animals, and it will increase the importance of you in your dog's life. She will be less likely to get mammary tumors, which can happen in female Jack's, and won't be able to develop uterine cancer. She won't have the medical complications due to pregnancy, and she won't aggressively protect her puppies. You won't have the financial burden of food and veterinary care for puppies, nor will you have the worry of finding them good homes.

Again, weigh the positives and the negatives carefully before you decide to breed. If you are a new breeder just starting out, it doesn't matter how many books you've read, you still need to learn good breeding practices and how important they are. A novice breeder who breeds one litter of puppies a year has the same responsibility for the welfare of those animals as any other breeder. The unfortunate truth of the matter is that many novice breeders often don't have the knowledge or the facilities to take care of the pups after they are born. These conditions make it hard to ensure that small breeding operations are producing healthy terriers. There are plenty of good tips to be found in books and magazines. The best form of knowledge is through hands on experience. Ask a breeder if they will let you take part in and help with their next litter of puppies so that you can determine if this is an activity that is right for you. Arrange for an experienced breeder to help you out and be present for at least your first litter of pups.

There are a number of important issues to consider about genetic science as it relates to dog breeding. A major concern that you should be clear on is the complications of in-breeding. If you are just beginning to breed litters be sure that you are serious in your commitment to the Jack Russell Terrier. There are three general areas that must be considered when you evaluate a pair of terriers in order to decide if each member of the pair should be bred and if so to decide if they should they be bred to each other: evaluate each terrier's outward appearance and temperament; study their pedigrees, and consider the degree and kind of inbreeding, if any, that you will allow with regard to our goal for the breeding.

First, it is important to look at the female as dispassionately as possible. What are her faults? Does she have any defects? Faults are aesthetic flaws while a defect is a genetic malformation or disease which can affect the dog's health, soundness, structure and/or temperament. Registered terriers must be veterinarian certified for soundness prior to registration, so it is unlikely that even the most novice breeder who has any care for the breed would consider breeding an individual who is defective. Unfortunately, possible defects can show up after a terrier is registered. Does your tough little dog show signs of back end lameness at the end of a long day in the field? Does your bitch chew her paws into a bloody mess in the fall? Situations like these can make for pretty tough decisions, especially for the novice breeder who owns a small number of treasured terriers.

The distinction between fault and defect is not always clear, especially when one is evaluating a working terrier. For the working Jack Russell, size, substance, eye shape, coat and of course, work style are directly related to function. Additionally hunting territory and quarry should also figure into your considerations. To complicate matters more, even among the more experienced breeders there is strong disagreement as to what constitutes a defect: some would not breed an animal with a level bite, others would not breed a terrier which stood too far back to bay, still others would not consider either of these characteristics to be defects of structure or temperament.

After you have decided that an individual terrier is, generally speaking, of the caliber to be bred, it then falls upon you to decide how to breed it. If you are just getting started, it is likely that you obtained your terrier from an experienced breeder. An experienced breeder can be a valuable resource. While you should know your terrier inside and out, your breeder should know the terrier's genetic history. The breeder should have tracked your dog's ancestors through a variety of breeding combinations, and thus will be able to tell you the sort of combination that will stand the greatest chance of producing puppies free of defects and conformational faults.

It's likely that every terrier, no matter how perfect its outward appearance, no matter what its breeding, carries the genetic potential for some sort of defect. A recessive gene for a given defect will only appear if it is paired with another recessive gene of the same sort. The experienced breeder who has proven stud dogs and a number of good brood bitches will have learned that crossing individuals with particular pedigrees will produce certain problems in the puppies. This does not necessarily mean that your breeder is going to tell you in detail about every genetic defect that their stock has experienced. Sometimes it is possible to determine which ancestor is responsible for a defect or fault. In the case of a defect avoid doubling up on that ancestor at all costs. Many times it is next to impossible for the breeder to determine which particular ancestor is responsible for a recessive gene. The breeder may, at the least, be able to advise you in general terms to avoid a cross, but will be unable to give you specific information as to why it should be avoided.

Being a novice breeder does not excuse you from taking responsibility for learning the genetic history of your animals. In order to prove you are a reliable and sensible breeder, you must develop knowledge of the pedigrees of an increasing number of terriers. You have the responsibility to inquire about the terriers you breed with and to follow up on the puppies you breed.

In selecting a stud dog it is recommended that you:
- Get a pedigree, see it, and don't just have it read to you over the phone.
- Send your pedigree to the owner of the stud dog. Ask if they have bred to familiar lines and if so, what the outcome was. Most important, were the puppies healthy and registerable? Then, what were the puppies' conformational characteristics?
- If the dog has never been put to your bitches lines, ask for the names of people who have bred to the stud dog, and then ask them about their litters. You should be particularly interested in the occurrence and rate of occurrence of problems and strengths common to the litters.

Finally it's important to consider the general goal of your breeding program with regard to the amount of inbreeding that this breeding will involve. When you look at the pedigree of the terriers you are considering for a cross, you will need to evaluate the degree of inbreeding the cross would involve. If the two have ancestors in common, you are considering inbreeding. The number of ancestors in common and their closeness to the breeding pair in the pedigree will determine the degree of inbreeding. You are considering a line breeding when you consider the pedigrees with the goal being to find a particular ancestor common to both individuals in order to increase the likelihood that the puppies will resemble that ancestor. Line breeding is a special form of inbreeding. When the pedigrees of a breeding pair show no ancestors in common within six generations then you are considering an out breeding.

Serious breeders, novice or not, should have a desire to produce outstanding individuals who will pass on their positive, dominant traits to their offspring. Some breeding programs involve higher degrees of inbreeding and can contribute to the appearance of an individual litter or line. The unhappy truth is that many inbreeding programs can also cause reduced fertility, increased health problems, and defects in other offspring. Any inbreeding program must include a certain amount of culling. In this case culling is done by spaying or neutering any and all pups of a litter that have defect or do not achieve the results that the breeder is aiming for. Often it is not that simple. Many inbred dogs will be weak, inferior, feeble, and live with constant suffering. In these cases it is advised that the dog be humanely euthanized. Also, culling does not necessarily involve a convenient spay/neuter contract and irresponsible breeders may pass a dog off as healthy which will taint any number of lines that it breeds with in the future.

The JRTCA will not accept any terrier that is inbred according to the JRTCA inbreeding definition. No father/daughter, mother/son, or brother/sister mating is permitted. Half brother/half sister mating is permitted only once within three generations if there is an ancestor that is common to both the sire and a dam. A generation is defined as the complete lineage of both the sire and the dam. Many novices don't realize that these rules still allow for relatively close inbreeding. Genetically speaking, the positive side of this is that increases the chances of producing those characteristics treasured in Jack Russell Terriers: intelligence, keen hunting ability, small chests, strong heads, good coats, happy, healthy warriors. The negative side of this is the increase in the chances of producing the genetic defects that are a breeder's worst nightmare. Above all you should choose to preserve, protect, and work a healthy Jack Russell Terrier.

There is a lot of work and luck involved in breeding a healthy set of puppies. Evaluating breeding stock, understanding pedigrees, and establishing worthwhile goals for a breeding program are activities that cannot be successfully carried out by an individual. It has to be a collaborative effort. Seek help from breeders and experts whenever possible. Working mutually with experts is a good investment towards building a successful bloodline free of genetic defect and illness.

Irish/Miniature Jack Russell Terriers

Anyone just learning about Jack Russell's and thinking about buying one should be aware that there is no recognized breed as the "Irish Jack Russell Terrier". Some breeders, who import short-legged Jack's from Ireland, have taken to calling their terriers

"Irish Jack Russell Terriers" or "Miniature Jack Russell Terriers". The breed does come in a wide variety of sizes, and a small one may appear mini compared to a large one, but a Jack Russell is a Jack Russell.

Whether they have long or short legs, all Jack Russell's have the same traits and legs have nothing to do with temperament or personality. A Jack Russell Terrier should be anywhere from 10-15 inches at the shoulders. They come in 3 coat types, smooth, broken and rough. They must be at least 51% white and the acceptable colors are black, tan, a combo called tri (black, tan and white). Any other colors are not acceptable. Some disreputable people try to pass off off-color dogs as "rare" or as "miniature" Jack Russell's. There is no such thing.

Many breeders will make claims that their terriers are bred to be great with small children, don't shed, and love cats. They are lying. The Jack Russell Terrier has been a hunting breed for over a hundred years and has very strong hunting instincts. They do shed and are normally not recommended for families with very small children. Different countries have their own "versions" of many things. Dogs referred to as "Irish Jack Russell's" don't look much like the dogs that fit the Jack Russell Terrier Club of Great Britain's breed standard, which is where the American standard came from. Short legs, broad chest, and big bones are the norm in this "type." Please review as many books, magazines and websites in your quest to learn about Jack Russell Terriers.

Chapter 8

The Health of the Jack Russell Terrier

In general the Jack Russell breed has a good reputation for being healthy and long-lived because of the strict protection breeders have exercised over the gene pool and prevention of direct in-breeding. When compared to other "showing" breeds of dog the Jack Russell has a much lower instance of in-breeding. Jack Russell's will live anywhere form 14-21 years on average if properly cared for. Although generally healthy for the most part, there are some specific health concerns that have been noticed in certain lines of Jack Russell and can appear in any line or generation because of recessive genetics.

Some Jack Russell specific health issues are:
- Hereditary Cataracts
- Primary Lens Luxation
- Congenital Deafness
- Medial Patellar Luxation
- Ataxia
- Legg-Calve-Perthes Disease
- Myasthenia Gravis
- Von Willebrand's Disease

A good breeder will avoid breeding a line that they believe may carry any of these illnesses through heredity. Good breeders will also have the puppies BAER tested for their hearing before any sales are made. All breeding pairs should be individually CERF tested and checked according to the Orthopedic Foundation for Animals standards before being bred in order to prevent passing on any hereditary eye or joint problems to the proposed litter. Enthusiasts are strongly urged not to by puppies that are bred form a breeding pair that is less than two years old. This is because some genetic illnesses may not have been noticed yet when a dog is under 2 years of age.

Caring for your Jack Russell

Please note that this information is provided as a rough overview and checklist of concerns to have tested. It should not be used in place of sound medical advice from your own veterinarian.

- **VISION**
    - CERF - Vision Testing
    - Cataracts, Distichiasis, Glaucoma, PLL, PRA
    - Primary Lens Luxation
    - Progressive Retinal Atrophy (PRA)
- **HEARING**
    - BAER- Hearing Testing
- **TOXICITY / POISONING**
    - ASPCA Help Line- **1-888-426-4435**
    - Avoid Skunks! – Their spray can be toxic to some Jacks and can cause convulsions, respiratory failure, facial ulcers and loss of consciousness.
    - Raisins! – These are toxic to Jack Russell's and will cause renal failure
    - http://www.terrier.com/breed/toxicity.php4 - a Guide to Possible Signs of Toxicity
    - Consult a listing of poisonous plants such as the one found at http://www.ansci.cornell.edu/plants/index.html so that you know which ones to try to keep your Jack away form.
- **BRAIN**
    - Coonhound Paralysis. A neurological paralysis that caused flaccid paralysis and loss of bladder control and respiratory function. Believe to be an immune response to an allergy to Raccoon saliva. Often follows a Raccoon bite.
    - Test for Canine Epilepsy
    - Watch for signs of Ataxia
- **HEART / BLOOD**
    - Sub-Aortic Stenosis - a fatal heart disease
    - Von Willebrand's Disease- inherited bleeding disorder
- **RESPIRATORY**
    - Kennel Cough- a mild self-limiting disease involving the trachea and bronchi of any age dog.
- **JOINTS**
    - Legg-Calve-Perthes Disease - a disease of the hip joints of small breeds of dogs
    - Medial Patellar Luxation - dislocation (slipping) of the patella (kneecap)
- **MISCELLANEOUS**
    - Always have a first aid kit handy when out in the field.

- o Be responsible to have these things done or checked. - Dental, Neutering, Vaccinations
- o Do not feed them or leave them unsupervised near the following: chocolate, alcohol, chicken or turkey bones, batteries, onions, garbage, medicines such as ibuprofen. These things are all dangerous or toxic and can cause illness or death.
- o Canine Ehrlichiosis - Tick borne disease that causes fever, chills, bleeding and other problems. Can be passed to humans.
- o http://netvet.wustl.edu/dogs.htm - extensive medical links

Spaying and Neutering

The basic personality and temperament of your Jack Russell Terrier will not be changed by removing his or her reproductive capability. Neutering a male can make him more tolerant of other males, but neither neutering nor spaying will by itself turn your dog lazy and obese. That is the result of excess food and insufficient exercise.

Advantages of Spaying Female Jack Russell

- You won't have the heat cycles that come every six months when your bitch goes into heat.
- There are many health problems that unspayed bitches can have.
- Lowers the chance of getting mammary tumors/cancer.
- You won't have to worry about male dogs jumping fences to get at your terrier.
- You won't have the worry about puppies you never wanted and mismatings that could be life threatening to her.

Veterinarians say it recommended that your girl get spayed before her first heat which normally occurs in this size bitch around 6 months of age. Spaying before the first heat will dramatically decrease her chances of mammary cancers and all sorts of female disorders.

Advantages of Neutering Male Jack Russell

- Early neutering can immensely decrease the likelihood of marking behavior.
- Can make him more tolerant of other males.
- Less tempted to escape or wander or be distracted from their family or work
- Will not develop testicular cancer, and the risk of prostate cancer is lowered.
- You won't have the worry about puppies you never wanted.

It's strongly recommended that you spay/neuter your Jack Russell unless you are planning to start a breeding program.

Please talk to your vet about spaying/neutering your terrier.

Anal Sacs

Anal sacs (sometimes referred to as anal glands) are located on either side of the anus at the 9 o'clock and 3 o'clock positions, where they are positioned just under the skin. They connect to the anus by means of small canals or ducts. Anal sacs produce and store a dark, foul-smelling fluid. Usually the dog will express these anal glands himself when taking a bowel movement. However, it is not uncommon for a dog to have to have his anal glands expressed by their vet or owner, on a regular basis, so that a problem does not occur.

There are 3 problems that occur in the anal sacs.
1. When the fluid becomes thick and solidified, the condition is called **impaction**.
2. When bacteria grow in this material producing yellow or bloody pus, the condition is called **infection**.
3. When the infection builds to create a hot, tender swelling in the sac, the condition is called an **abscess**. When the abscessed material overflows the sac, the skin over the sac breaks open, and the pus drains onto the skin.

Symptoms of anal sac problems include:
1. Scooting or dragging the anal area.
2. Excessive licking under the tail.
3. Pain, sometimes severe, near the tail or anus.
4. A swollen area on either side of the anus.
5. Bloody or sticky drainage on either side of the anus.

If you notice any of these symptoms, it's best to make an appointment with your veterinarian to have it checked out. The vet will be able to explain to you further about the anal sacs and show you how to express them. If you are not comfortable expressing them yourself at home, you may need to take the dog back to the vet at the most once a week to have this done. Doing this can prevent infection, impaction, or possible abscess of the anal glands.

Vomiting
There are several dogs out there that will vomit if their stomach is empty for too long. It's not uncommon. If you are feeding once a day, try feeding twice a day. If your terrier is vomiting early morning, try giving a treat late at night before bed or feeding first thing in the morning. Sometimes you'll need to split the feedings to three to four times a day for a dog with a very sensitive stomach. If this doesn't work, definitely discuss it with your vet. There may be another underlying gastrointestinal problem such as ulcers, bacteria growth, pancreatitis, etc.

Skunk - Odors and Treatment below ground
If you can't find a good odor remover at your local pet store the best home remedy is: A mixture of one quart hydrogen peroxide, one-fourth cup baking soda & 2 T Dawn dishwashing detergent (mix together, scrub dog down; leave on dog for several minutes, rinse with warm water). **Caution: do not store mixture in a sealed container (mixture gives off vapors and pressure may explode container).**
If your dog is sprayed underground; assess the situation. Once the dog is out, whether dug to or out on his own volition, examine him. Look at his overall appearance. Is he having difficulty walking/standing? Is he throwing up? What color are his gums? Looking at a dog's gums gives you an idea of the status of his circulation. As shock progresses gums will go from healthy pink, to pale pink, to white, to blue-purple. This is

a reflection of the body shunting blood away from non-vital peripheral tissues. In advanced shock the gums are bluish because the oxygen in the blood remaining in this tissue has been used up. If you are not familiar with the appearance of normal gums, look at your dog's gums so you will be. A dogs whose gums are slightly pale, vomits once or twice and is having a LITTLE difficulty walking will likely recover completely within a few minutes. This behavior is typical of a dog that has been sprayed but gets out of the hole quickly. Let the dog rest and allow small drinks of water. Keep a close eye on the dog - he should recover to normal behavior and gums should return to a healthy pink within about 30 minutes or less. The dog should be seen by a veterinarian if full recovery is not achieved or if he seems to recover but then deteriorates. The dog that has been trapped in a hole and/or sprayed in the face is more likely to be in serious condition. Gums may be very pale or blue-purple; the dog may be staggering or unable to stand, may be staring blankly and may vomit several times. This dog should receive veterinary care IMMEDIATELY. Treat the areas of the skin which have been sprayed as soon as possible, but DO NOT delay getting to a vet. Treat the areas of skin which have been sprayed as soon as possible with water, then a skunk odor product or the solution above.

When contacting a vet you may have to insist the dog be seen immediately. Tell the vet the circumstances, that the dog was down in a hole when sprayed and could not escape from the fumes, and that you know of dogs in similar situations that have died because they went into shock. Tell the veterinarian what color the dog's gums are, if he is having difficulty walking/standing, if he is staring blankly and how many times he has vomited. This information will help the vet understand that the dog really is in serious condition. Wherever you are hunting, and whoever you are hunting with, make sure there is a vet within thirty minutes in case of emergency.

BAER Testing

BAER stands for **Brainstem Auditory Evoked Response**. This test records brain responses to click sounds delivered to an ear. It does not require a behavioral response from the animal, hence no chance of misinterpretation of a dog's response. The test can be done quickly, and will give a definitive record of each ear's response to sound. The BAER is currently being used to eliminate or reduce the incidence of genetic expression of deafness from several breeds of dogs. Since deafness is a genetic defect, and since it appears essentially at 2-3 weeks of age, testing the pup anytime after 5 weeks of age with the BAER has become an excellent way to identify the auditory status of individual dogs. This deafness trait has not been observed to develop gradually in dogs, and does seem to be an all-or-none situation for each ear.

- Bilateral - deaf in both ears (i.e., totally deaf)
- Unilateral - deaf in one ear (often called "unis")

Here are some basic steps that responsible Jack Russell Terrier breeders can take to reduce deafness in Jack Russell's.

1. BAER tests all breeding stock and never breeds a totally deaf or unilaterally deaf individual.
2. BAER tests all litters of puppies before they leave your kennel to go to new homes.
3. Avoid repeating a breeding that produces deafness.

4. Responsible stud dog owners should never breed to a bitch that has not been BAER tested.
5. In most cases, do not place or keep a totally deaf individual. It takes a VERY special person to raise and train a deaf dog and the club does not recommend it because of everything it involves. Fear biting is just one of many problems. However, there are books on the subject that can help an owner train a deaf terrier.
6. Seek normal pet homes for unilaterally deaf puppies but insist on them being spayed or neutered at the earliest suitable age and NEVER provide pedigree and stud certificate paperwork that is not clearly marked that the individual is unilaterally deaf.

BAER Testing Clinics
- Cornell University Vet School, Ithaca, NY
- Animal Medical Center, NY, NY
- Tufts University, Boston area, MA
- Auburn University in Auburn, Alabama
- Veterinary School at the University of Missouri in Columbia, MO

CERF Testing

CERF (**Canine Eye Registration Foundation**) was founded by a group of concerned purebred owner/breeders with a goal of eliminating heritable eye diseases in purebred dogs through registration, research, and education. CERF is dedicated to educating the public on matters involving canine eye disease. It provides a variety of reports to help educate owners and breeders on heritable eye disease questions, healthy breeding stock, and breed-specific eye problems.

The Genetics Committee of the American College of Veterinary Ophthalmologists lists Lens Luxation and Cataracts in its Occular Disorders Presumed to be Inherited in Purebred Dogs for the Jack Russell Terrier. Occurrence of a defect cannot be anticipated in a given terrier, and the age of onset of the disorder(s) varies from quite early (less than one year of age) to several years of age. The JRTCA Breeder's Committee is urging terrier owners to have their Jack Russell's CERF tested yearly. Don't be fooled into waiting for a symptom of an eye problem. Many times there are none. Early detection and reporting is important to the future of the Jack Russell Terrier.

CERF Certification Process
1. Go to a board-certified canine ophthalmologist for the CERF exam
2. The CERF form is completed by the doctor
    o one copy for you
    o one copy for examining vet
    o one copy for CERF
3. Test results are sent to CERF for inclusion in its database
4. Fill out the reverse side of your copy
5. Enclose check and mail to CERF
6. CERF will send you a registration certification number in a few weeks

7. Keep certificate with your dog's portfolio with pedigree, JRTCA registration, and BAER test readout
8. Your name and your dog's name will be added to the list of certified dogs for that year. At year's end, the list is sent to all CERF members.

The official certificate (along with your BAER results) shows that you have made every effort to insure that your breeding stock is healthy and sound.

To register your dog with CERF or to have your canine eye health questions answered, contact CERF at:
CERF
1242 Lynn Hall
Purdue University
W. Lafayette, IN 47907
(765) 494-8179
(765) 494-9981 (fax)
CERF Web Site:

Health care tips for the Working Jack Russell Terrier
1. Feed your terrier plenty of high quality dog food. Don't skimp and try to save money by feeding a cheap, low protein, high fat food.
2. Feed your terrier the morning you hunt him and take at least half-ration to give him at noon if he has been working all morning. Sending a terrier into the field without breakfast can be dangerous as his sugar level drops and he potentially approaches hypoglycemia.
3. Make sure your terrier is fit before taking him in the field. A fit terrier is definitely NOT a thin terrier. Fitness has to do with muscle tone and staying power, neither of which your terrier can attain if he is thin.
4. If you hunt your terrier in the ice and snow, periodically check the pads of his feet and in between his toes for cuts, abrasions, and signs of frost bite.
5. Don't expect your terrier to be able to brave the severe winter cold or extreme summer heat if he is a house mouse 24 hours a day.
6. Make sure your terrier is current on all of his vaccinations. Spending a few extra dollars on annual rabies and Lyme vaccinations may save your terriers life.
7. After the hunt, flush your terrier's eyes with plenty of sterile water and check to make sure there are no pieces of grit left in his eyes. It is a good idea to follow the eye wash with an anti-bacterial eye ointment such as Terramycin eye ointment. Check the eyes the next morning for signs of grit you may have missed, and if necessary, flush the eyes again and follow with a sterile eye ointment.
8. Make sure your hunting pack is complete. Take along a knife, limb saw, flash light, tea bags (family size--wet them and hold tightly over a laceration; the bleeding will stop in a few minutes), post hole diggers, large and small shovels, a

metal bar, towels and blankets to wrap your terrier in, plenty of fresh water, extra batteries for your collars and box, and an extra collar and box if you have one.

9. It's a good idea to have a cellular phone and the telephone numbers of several vets in the area. A cell-phone and a local vet may save your terrier's life if he gets into skunk many miles from home!

10. Remember, prepare for the worst, and expect the best. Your terrier depends upon you for safety; you depend on your terrier for everything else.

Chapter 9

Is the Jack Russell Terrier the right dog for you? Pros and Cons

These feisty little Terriers capture the hearts of many, but that doesn't mean that they are the dog meant for everyone. They may not even be the dog meant for you. While adaptable to a variety of environments, they are first and foremost bred to be hunting dogs. City or apartment living, or a confined or sedate lifestyle, does not suit a Jack Russell. Special facilities and handling are absolutely necessary, especially when owning two or more Jack Russell's. You must be ready to provide firm, consistent and responsible training and discipline. While facilitating outdoor activity and exercise is essential, you can never leave your Jack Russell Terrier unattended, even in the country. The courage of the Jack Russell means it may take on any adversary twice their size or more. They are intelligent, determined, and bold, but sometimes you have to apply the brakes that they weren't built with.

You may find the antics of the Jack Russell amusing, but don't forget they are also assertive and feisty. A well looked after Jack Russell Terrier is a happy, bold, energetic dog, extremely loyal, intelligent, and assertive. Their greatest attribute is their working ability, closely followed by their excellent qualities as a companion. Their funny antics will continually amuse you and their intelligence knows no bounds, although their assertive nature and boundless energy can at times be overwhelming. No matter what you see on TV, these little dogs are not "Wishbone". These dogs require an extraordinary amount of human attention, outdoor activity, exercise, discipline, and your understanding and acceptance. Their natural instinct may make them aggressive towards other small animals such as snakes, cats, gerbils, guinea pigs. They can also be very aggressive with other dogs. Never leave more than two together unattended. Even young pups must be carefully monitored. Their aggressiveness is a part of their specifically bred nature.

There is a handy resource online at www.terrier.com to see if a Jack Russell is the right dog for you. Many experienced, as well as inexperienced, dog owners are overwhelmed by the demands of a Jack Russell Terrier, leading to the dogs being abandoned even before they reach adulthood. Jack Russell's are first and foremost hunting dogs. The traits and skills that make them excellent hunting dogs (i.e., digging, barking, aggressive nature, ability to follow scent) are often interpreted as bad habits that cause people to give them up.

These dogs are bred to go underground, following scent to locate and bark at quarry until they are dug down to or the quarry bolts. If they do not have an outlet for their natural instincts, they will invent new and fun jobs for themselves, which frequently include guardian of the world and/or their possessions and family, chasing cars, hunting birds, bugs or leaves, or endlessly digging in the soil.

Jack Russell's are often described as a big dog in a little body. They have the same need for exercise as a much larger dog, possibly even more so. They have the mentality of a much larger dog. They think they are at least 150 pounds, and are fearless, often challenging other dogs three times their size. Jacks can often be aggressive with other dogs. Same-sex aggression and aggression towards other breeds of dogs is well documented with this terrier. It is strongly recommended that no more than two Jack Russell's, of opposite sex, ever be permitted to stay together unattended.

No matter what you heard form Aunt Gloria Jack Russell Terriers are not a non-shedding breed! All coat types shed! Smooth coats shed the most, dropping hair continuously year round. Rough coats maintain the guard and dead coat, requiring manual shedding a few times a year. The broken coat is an intermediary coat, between the two types.

If you own a Jack it will require firm, consistent discipline. They are extremely intelligent; continue to test their limits throughout their life. More often than not, train their owners before the owner knows what has happened. This ability to train their owners can include displays of aggressive behavior. Their assertive nature must be understood and handled properly. The Jack Russell can become very possessive of their owner or a favorite member of the family or of what they consider to be their personal property if allowed to do so to the point of showing aggressive protective behavior that must be controlled from an early age.

Jack's that are not accustomed to other types of animals form an early age are commonly known to harass, injure or kill other small pets, such as cats, birds, rabbits, mice, rats, etc., simply due to their strong natural hunting instinct. Always be careful. Hunting instincts can come into play any time and raising a puppy with a cat does not guarantee the cat's life-long safety.

A healthy and cared for Jack Russell will remain active well into their 15-year-plus life span; their need for activity and desire to hunt continues for their entire lifetime. Untrained, unsupervised dogs rarely meet their life expectancy. Your Jack will require at least basic obedience training. The dog's life may depend on it. Even well trained dogs will be tempted to chase something interesting, or even disappear into a hole while you are not looking. Off-lead is always a dangerous situation for a Jack Russell unless in a safe environment with experienced Jack Russell owners.

Owners of Jack Russell Terriers absolutely need a securely fenced yard. Jack Russell's will roam due to their hunting instincts even if left in an unsecured for a few minutes! You can let them out every day with no trouble, but eventually they will disappear and may never come back. They can also dig under, climb, or jump over fences; some can climb trees and any height chain link fencing. A Jack Russell will be very destructive if left unattended and bored. Most behavioral problems are due to a lack of companionship, discipline, activity, and exercise. If you've only seen perfect, well-behaved Jack's, they are the lucky ones with responsible owners.

Jack Russell's are best suited to rural life. When made to live in a city or suburban-type environment, their needs and instincts do not change. It would be unreasonable to expect them to be anything other than what they are genetically bred to be. Your lifestyle must be adjusted to meet their needs; they must have an outlet for their considerable energy and intelligence. Experts do not recommend Jack Russell's as apartment or condo dogs. They need a great deal of exercise and outdoor activity, and are usually too loud for such high-density living. They need room to run; leash walking does not satisfy their boundless energy. Unless your schedule permits many hours at home and a lot of outdoor activity, with a safe place the terrier can run, this is not the dog for you. Many rescue dogs came from apartments, condos, or homes where the owners work away from the home for long periods of time.

A Jack Russell will not stand for any mistreatment from a child. They will not put up with typical child handling such as pulling of ears, taking or "sharing" of the dog's bones, food, toys, etc. They are very assertive and demanding, and will be jumping all over whoever will allow it. Jack Russell's are not recommended for households with children under the age of six unless you are previously experienced with the breed.

Jacks are not as they are portrayed in the movies, on TV, or other forms of media. Those dogs are professionally trained and handled, and are very obedient only for very short periods of time. These are tasks that the Jack has been retrained to recognize as work, utilizing their natural work instincts. Celebrity dogs have their needs met by the trainer, and perform their jobs because they know they will be rewarded afterward.

Jack Russell Terriers require a long-term commitment to obedience, activity, and exercise. Their high energy level can frustrate you, entertain you, and can bring you happiness and grief. If this type of relationship does not appeal to you, then consider another breed. Your Jack Russell will always be a work in progress.

Dirt, Dirt and more Dirt

Jack Russell Terriers are bred to go underground, following scent of prey. If they do not have an outlet for their natural instincts, they will soon be chasing cars, hunting birds, bugs or leaves, or endlessly digging up your garden.

Bathing and Shedding

After getting dirty, Jack Russell Terriers are not overly fond of taking a bath. Usually a warm water rinse and a towel dry are good enough. If you do use a shampoo be sure to use a gentle one. You do not want to bathe them too often as it can lead to dry skin. Be aware that Jack Russell's will shed. All coat types shed.

Crate Training

A Jack Russell Terriers should always be crate trained. They can be very destructive if left unattended. Most behavioral problems are due to a lack of companionship and discipline

Love to Dig

Jack Russell Terriers love to dig. Say goodbye to your flower bed.

Breeding

Jack Russell Terriers make wonderful parents. However, breeding is risky business and should not be undertaken lightly. Breeders should follow a strict code of ethics, have their breeding stock BAER and CERF tested, and breed only to registered dogs

Jack Russell's Around the Globe

Jack Russell Terriers can be found throughout the world. There are large concentrations of the breed in the United States, Great Britain, Canada, Australia, Sweden, South Africa and many other countries.

Many experienced, as well as inexperienced, dog owners are overwhelmed by the demands of a Jack Russell Terrier, leading many dogs to be abandoned to animal shelters before they reach their first year. Any potential owners should carefully weigh the information available and use their best judgment to decide if a dog like the Jack Russell is right for them. As mentioned previously, there is a profiler available online that should be used as the first step to realistically see if your lifestyle is compatible with the addition of a Jack Russell. The recommendations of the Profiler are based upon the "Bad Dog" brochure which has been one of the JRTCA's primary written education tools for potential owners and breeders. Many of the recommendations generated by the Profiler are phrased as absolutes and generalities, however, in real life, nothing is absolute. Each Jack Russell Terrier is unique.

Reading the chapter above and using the JRTCA's online profiler may discourage many interested dog lovers form owning a Jack. Often, this turns out best for the health and well being of the Jack Russell Terrier. Although we all want to be happy and love and cuddle a fuzzy little friend without considering potential problems, it's in the dog's best interests to be honest with yourself and about the characteristics of the breed. There are far too many Jack Russell's depending on rescue shelters for their survival because they were originally purchased by owners who were not prepared for them. Many did not realize the unique requirements and characteristics of the Jack Russell Terrier. Please use as much time, research and honest consideration as is needed before you make your final decision of whether or not you want to add a Jack Russell to your home.

Chapter 10

Famous Jack Russell Terriers

Despite all the cautions and arguments to be made against prospective owners buying a Jack Russell thinking that they're going to get the kind of dog they see on TV, behaving and looking cute; you can't help but fall in love with the ones who do appear on screen. Some dogs will find fame and become endeared tot the hearts of the public in other ways. No matter the reasoning, be it through Hollywood or public bravery, here are some of the world's most famous Jack Russell's who will always have a home in the hearts of people around the world.

Krypto the Superdog

Okay, although this first one is a fictitious character, it is no less interesting. Krypto was introduced as a character in the Superman comics of the 1960's. Krypto is a white terrier type breed that was the sole canine survivor of the planet Krypton and because of a strange time/space vortex did not arrive on Earth until much later than

Superman. Krypto quickly became a popular recurring character and an unofficial part time sidekick of Superman. Since then Krypto has earned popularity all of his own. Krypto has gone on to establish his own spin-off of the Superman franchise and today is featured in his own toys, books, games, comics, and even his own Saturday morning cartoon. Although there's been no official word on his breed, since he is supposed to be from Krypton, it is still open; but it has been said that original concept for the character was based on a Jack Russell Terrier from a line of smooth coated Jack's that was all white in color.

Moose

Moose is best known as the canine actor who played "Eddie" on the popular TV show Fraser, a spin-off of the classic Cheers sitcom. Moose's expert timing and comical facial features made him one of the most popular actors on the show. Moose was also the star of the classic children's movie "My Dog Skip" starring Frankie Muniz. As if TV and Film weren't enough, Moose was also the lucky Jack Russell that parachuted into the half-time show with Seinfeld star Jason Alexander during the 1996 Super bowl.

Enzo

Enzo is the wiry haired look-a-like son of Moose. As his father began to age and the stunts became too demanding for him Enzo stood in for him in the more challenging scenes on both Fraser and in "My Dog Skip".

Soccer

Although you likely won't know Soccer by his real name, if you a parent of a child in the late 90's you probably know him by his stage name, also the title of his popular children's show, Wishbone. As Wishbone, Soccer has entertained millions of children worldwide and easily earned a reputation as one of the world's most intelligent dogs. Soccer has gone to great lengths in the name of entertainment, even dressing up in costume and acting out classic stories; all the while bringing the unique personality and life of the Jack Russell to the screen.

Max VI

Max the Jack Russell is one of those dogs who just can't escape his nature, and spends most of his time running and playing like any Jack Russell. That's probably why he's only done two movies in his career, but he's not complaining. Max played a female dog named Audrey in the 2000 movie Mr. Accident. Max's other role is one of the most beloved Jack Russell roles in modern film. Max was played the role of Milo in the Jim Carrey Blockbuster "The Mask". Not only did Max get to do the traditional plot foils normally reserved for an energetic Jack Russell on a movie set, he stole the show, and in one screen got to step into the starring role when he stole the magical mask from his owner and was able to wreak havoc both in the film and on set as a spinning tornado of a Jack Russell possessed by the god of mischief. Very fitting.

Chalky

Chalky enjoyed being one of the most recognizable canine stars of the UK, and he didn't even have to act or use a different name. That's because he's the pet of famous television Chef Rick Stein. Stein has starred in several short lived cooking shows, and always had Chalky at his side, even while cameras were rolling. This little fur ball became so beloved by the people of Britain that it even led to his own merchandising including kitchen ware, toys, dog accessories, art print, home accessories and more. Chalky even has his own beer named after him.

Tillamook Cheddar

Tillamook Cheddar is a very original Jack Russell. She appeared in the movie "Tillie goes BUST", but what this canine star from Brooklyn is best known for is her art. Tillie, for short, is one of the most famous and renowned animal artists in the world. She has been painting using her own unique style since she was a pup and has displayed an amazing ability to learn basic techniques and use of color. Tillie has appeared on a number of late night talk shows displaying her unique talents.

Barkley

This is the perfect name for such a feisty and hard working actor. With a talent this giant, no wonder his owners named him after the massive dog character from Sesame Street. Barkley recently appeared in the 2003 movie "the Little Magician" where he plays a dog that can work magic. Prior to that role he starred on TV shows such as Burke's law and as "Baby" the 1994 film "Clean Slate" starring comedian Dana Carvey. Barkley's most famous role was his first big break as "Rimshot", the loving sidekick the Jim Varney's "Ernest" character in "Earnest Scared Stupid and Earnest Goes to Jail".

Skippy

Skippy was the most famous Hollywood dog of the 1930's and 40's. Skippy got his first big break as "George", starring with Cary Grant and Katherine Hepburn in the 1938 film "Bringing up Baby". Skippy also starred as "Mr. Smith" in the 1937 film "The Awful Truth". A year after "Bringing up Baby", Skippy again starred with Cary Grant as a dog named "Mr. Atlas" in the film "Topper Takes a Trip". Skippy's next role would propel him further into the limelight when he landed the role of "Asta" in the Thin-Man series of franchise films starring along with Myrna Lo and William Powell.

George

This dog never appeared in a movie or TV show, but he is now considered a national hero in New Zealand. On April 29th of 2007, a group of five small children were attacked by a pair of Pit Bull's that had been wandering loose. One of the children was accompanied by a Jack Russell Terrier named George. As the Pit Bulls attacked the children George charge at them and fought them off. The animals had been abandoned by the owner and were known to be vicious, often terrorizing the neighborhood. It's speculated that the original owners had purposely trained them to be cross and aggressive to use for protection and in dog fighting.

George fought bravely against the huge, savage dogs, and held them back long enough for the children to escape. Unfortunately George would have to sacrifice himself to save the children and was wounded beyond medical treatment. George would have to be humanely euthanized in due to his injuries. The New Zealand SPCA posthumously awarded the medal of bravery to George, something usually only done for humans. A former U.S. marine now living in New Zealand even donated his own Purple Heart medal, which he had received for brave service in Vietnam, to George's owner.

Other Famous Jack's

Some Jack's aren't famous for any of the above reasons, but just because their parents are. Just as with regular people, Jack Russell's are also popular with celebrities who love animals.

Just a few of the celebrities who are or have been Jack Russell fans are:
- Paul McCartney
- Goldie Hawn
- Mariah Carey
- Bette Midler
- Serena Williams
- Charlotte Church
- Camilla Parker-Bowles

Even Prince Charles is known to have a number of Jack Russell's

In the end, whether a Jack Russell is famous for being on TV, movies, an artist, for bravery, or for being owned by a star; the entire breed has used its amazing intelligence and work ethic to become a shining star of the dog world, and we know that to each of us our own unique Jack Russell's are a star in our own hearts.

Glossary

An explanation of Jack Russell Terms

- **Affiliate** - a local club whose purpose is to provide activities for, and communication between JR enthusiasts within a local geographic area.
- **Agility** - a trial event in which dogs traverse a maze of obstacles and compete for speed and accuracy.
- **AKC** (American Kennel Club) - the JRTCA is opposed to any form of all-breed registry or kennel recognition of the Jack Russell Terrier
- **BAER** (Brainstem Auditory Evoked Response) - a test being used to eliminate or reduce the incidence of genetic expression of deafness from several breeds of dogs.
- **Bilateral Deafness** - inability to hear; i.e., completely deaf, both ears affected.
- **Brindle** - a particular type of coat marking characterized by a pattern of black and brown; it is considered a registration fault.
- **Broken Coat** - a coat that is very similar to a smooth coat but has trace hair on the head, face, legs or body. A broken coat needs minimal alterations to be ready for the show ring. They will generally only require a quick tidying up. A broken coat should not be soft - it should be harsh to provide protection from the elements.

- **Bronze Medallion** - a special honor given by the JRTCA to those Jack Russell's and their owners who have earned three (or more) Natural Hunting Certificates Below Ground to different quarry.
- **CERF** (Canine Eye Registration Foundation) - a group of concerned purebred owner/breeders with a goal of eliminating heritable eye diseases in purebred dogs through registration, research, and education.
- **Cerebellar Ataxia** - degeneration of the cortex of the cerebellum leading to a staggering gait; it may or may not progress.
- **COE** (Code of Ethics) - The Breeders Code of Ethics outlines the ethical breeding practices expected of all JRTCA members.
- **Conformation** - a trial event in which the terrier is judged on the degree in which various angles and parts of the body agree or harmonize with each other (based on a breed standard). In addition to conformation and movement, the dog is judged on temperament; as in all things having to do with Jack Russell's, the best working dog is being sought.
- **Cross Entering** - the act of entering your terrier in multiple conformation classes at a terrier trial (i.e., between the open and miscellaneous division)
- **Dam** - the mother of a dog.
- **Dishing** - fault action of a foreleg when a toe is thrown outward in a circular movement; it is considered a registration fault
- **Go-to-Ground** - a trial event designed to simulate and test a Jack Russell's ability to hunt and work underground.
- **Hocks** - the ankle joint.
- **Inbreeding** - a breeding technique which pairs closely related animals, such as father-daughter, brother-sister, or cousins. Inbreeding favors genes of excellence as well as deleterious genes.
- **Incisors** - the front teeth; in a dog there are a total of six upper and lower incisors.
- **Jack** – Nickname for Jack Russell Terrier breed
- **JRT** – Nickname for Jack Russell Terrier breed
- **JRTC** – A generic term for any Jack Russell Terrier club, usually based regionally by state or country.
- **JRTAA** (Jack Russell Terrier Association of America) - now known as the Parson Russell Terrier Association of America (PRTAA); formerly the Jack Russell Terrier Breeders Association (JRTBA); a small breed club that has pushed for AKC recognition of the Jack Russell Terrier against the wishes of the JRTCA; the JRTAA is considered a conflicting organization. (**info**)
- **JRTCA** (Jack Russell Terrier Club of America) - the largest Jack Russell Terrier club and registry in the world; the National Breed Club and Registry for the Jack Russell Terrier in the United States. (**info**)
- **JRTCC** – Jack Russell Terrier Club of Canada.
- **JRTCB** – Jack Russell Terrier Club of Great Britain.
- **Legg Perthes** - Aseptic necrosis of the head and neck of the femur causes rear leg lameness; it is a disease of the hip joints of small breeds of dogs.
- **Lens Luxation** - dislocation of the lens from its normal site behind the cornea (partial or complete).
- **Level Bite** - the incisors meet cusp tip to cusp tip rather than have the uppers overlap the lowers (see scissor bite). This is an acceptable bite for a Jack Russell Terrier.
- **Natural Hunting Certificate (NHC)** - awarded for natural earthwork by the terrier and owner, judged by a sanctioned working judge, and is issued to only JRTCA registered or recorded dogs.

- **Off-Lead** - the act of running your terrier through an agility course without a leash. The terrier is controlled with hand and voice signals.
- **On-Lead** - the act of running your terrier through an agility course on a leash. After on-lead agility is mastered, the owner and terrier move to off-lead.
- **Over Bite** - a condition where the upper jaw is longer than the lower jaw. This is an unacceptable bite for a Jack Russell Terrier.
- **Patella** - the kneecap
- **Patellar Luxation** - dislocation of the kneecap; can be inherited or acquired through trauma
- **Plaiting** - action when the terrier's feet cross over each other; it is considered a registration fault
- **Prick Ears** - a condition where the ears of a Jack Russell Terrier stick straight up; considered a registration fault.
- **Progressive Retinal Atrophy** - degeneration of the retinal vision cells which progresses to blindness.
- **Refusal** - when a terrier "commits" (places one foot on the obstacle) and fails to continue to perform on the obstacle in agility.
- **Rough Coat** - a coat that has excess trace hair on the head, face, legs or body. The hair is longer than on a smooth or broken coat. A rough coat requires more alterations than a broken coat to be ready for the show ring. A rough coat should not be soft or wooly - it should be harsh to provide protection from the elements.
- **Sanctioned Trial** - a terrier trial whose format is approved and sanctioned by the JRTCA.
- **Scissor Bite** (Incisor Overlap) - the upper incisors overlap the lower incisors. This is the recommended bite for a Jack Russell Terrier.
- **Short or "High" Toes** - this is a developmental condition where the outside toes, usually on one or both front feet, do not grow to normal length, giving the appearance of being a "short" or "high" toe that does not touch the ground when full the terrier is full grown.
- **Sire** - the father of a dog.
- **Span** - the act of placing average size hands around the widest part behind the shoulders of the terrier; a small chest allows the terrier to follow his quarry down narrow earths
- **Smooth Coat** - a coat that does not have trace hair on the head, face, legs or body. A smooth coat does not require any alterations to be ready for the show ring. The coat should not be sparse or soft - it should provide protection from the elements.
- **State Representative** - JRTCA members throughout the U.S. that provide information on the breed and the Club and act as liaison for members in their respective areas.
- **Stifle** - the knee.
- **Stop** - the point between a dog's eyes between the crown and the muzzle; the dip on the forehead.
- **Terrier** - The name terrier is derived from the French 'terre', meaning earth. The terrier's role is not to fight with its quarry, but to locate it underground and to bark at it continuously, either causing it to leave the earth or alternatively to indicate where in the earth the quarry is located – in order that it can be dug to.
- **Trace Hair** - uncontrollable lengths of hair that does not lie close to the body.

- **Trial Certificate** - awarded to Jack Russell's which achieve a 100 percent score in the Open Class of the Go-to-Ground Division at a JRTCA sanctioned trial.
- **True Grit** - the official magazine of the JRTCA; published bimonthly to all members.
- **Umbilical Hernia** - Outpouching of skin over belly button; may contain abdominal viscera, and regress spontaneously.
- **Under Bite** - a condition where the lower jaw is longer than the upper jaw. This is an unacceptable bite for a Jack Russell Terrier.
- **Unilateral Deafness** - partial deafness; one ear affected.
- **UKC** (United Kennel Club) - an all breed registry of dogs.
- **Veterinary Certificate** - designed specifically for the Jack Russell Terrier, this form must be completed and signed by a licensed veterinarian (**within 30 days of application**) stating that he has examined the terrier and found it to be free from inherited defects. Required for registration.
- **Withers** - the spot above the shoulders; the base of the neck.
- **Wobbler Syndrome** - abnormality of the neck vertebrae causing rear leg ataxia which may progress to paralysis.
- **Wry** - A wry mouth or wry bite occurs when one side of the jaw grows more than the other.

Made in the USA
Lexington, KY
06 June 2010